SIR GEOFFREY VICKERS

Value Systems
and
Social Process

BASIC BOOKS, INC., PUBLISHERS

New York

For Ellen
in love and gratitude

To know can only wonder breede
And not to know is wonder's seede.
                    Sidney Godolphin, 1610–1643

Contents

Foreword

The theme of this book is the process by which men and societies develop and change the values by which they live.

The viewpoint is that of one who is sharply aware that our species has emerged from the evolutionary stream in what is, biologically, a very brief time; who, in consequence is daily surprised at the extent to which we have become differentiated even from our fellow primates the chimpanzees; and who is correspondingly interested in those possibilities and limitations which are peculiar to human kind.

The context is one of threat, arising from a self-generated rate and direction of change with which our species seems ill equipped to cope, either biologically or culturally.

The conceptual approach is one which accords high importance to human communication as a creative agent and finds in new developments of communication science some basis for a qualified hope, though not for the hopes most commonly entertained.

The first three papers are concerned with what I have called the ecology of ideas. The concepts and values with which we select and interpret experience are often regarded by science as mere derivatives of biological needs or instinctual drives. Yet even if they were no more than this, they would still be potent determinants of human behaviour in their own right during those times when changing circumstances have left them inept to our needs; and during times of continuous change this might be their normal condition, as indeed, it clearly is now. The view here taken credits them with somewhat greater autonomy, as products of human

xi

communication. 'Like the life forms of the physical world, the
dreams of men spread and colonize their inner world, clash, excite,
modify, and destroy each other, or preserve their stability by
making strange accommodations with their rivals' (p. 32). So I
regard it as a legitimate analogy, though not, of course, an exact
one, to speak of our interpretative system – I call it an appreciative
system – as an ecological system, even though the laws which
order and develop a population of ideas (conflicting, competing,
and mutually supporting) in communicating minds are different
from those which order and develop a population of monkeys in a
rain forest or of insects under a paving stone.

Of these three papers, the first seeks to disentangle some of the
ideas about progress which only a century ago seemed to provide
a coherent framework for Western man's thinking about his
nature and his destiny. In its heyday this system of thought
provided an example of an appreciative system as comprehensive
and coherent as anything the West had known since the medieval
age of faith. Its surviving fragments haunt and confuse us today,
in our attempt to replace it by something more apt to the condition in which it has left us.

The second paper seeks to relate the course of events and the
course of ideas over a wider span of space and time and to suggest
what a science of *human* ecology would have to comprise, if it
were to do justice to the degree of autonomy enjoyed by the
shared world of concepts and values in which, as creatures
humanized by communication, we effectively live.

The third paper, describing our present state of development
as the impending end of 'free fall', explores the political and social
repercussions of that august event; the changes, chosen or imposed
by man or circumstance, which it is likely to involve in the ways
we structure and value our situation.

Together, these three papers describe the world crisis both as
the closing of an ecological trap and as a failure of communication,
between nations, between governments and governed, and between
the generations. This crisis is conceived as due not to any lack of

means to transmit, store, and process information (which already far exceed what we can use) but to the absence or breakdown of those shared systems of interpretation by which alone communications have meaning and enable human beings to influence each other. And this failure is found to be due partly to the far more difficult tasks which communication is being required to perform and partly to the eroding of one interpretative system by another.

The papers in the second part ('The Tower of Babel') explore further the problems of governing any society in these conditions; in particular, the dilemma involved in making and in implementing choices which become ever more multi-valued and which involved collective action ever more widely extended and more closely integrated over space and time. In this connection they consider the hopes – and fears – to be attached to contemporary attempts to apply system analysis and system design to the political process. The third of these papers explores from a more psychological angle the process of multi-valued choice, whether collective or individual, and thus leads to the papers which form the third part.

These last are concerned with the scentific status of the views implicit in earlier papers and with their relation, on the one hand to the huge body of shared assumptions about human behaviour which is implicit in our language and culture and, on the other, to the physical and biological sciences.

For the psycho-social sciences operate in a domain which is still imperfectly related both to the world of tradition and experience and to the natural order as science has hitherto conceived it. Those who want – as I do – to accommodate our experience of human life within our idea of the natural order without cramping the one or bursting the other, must make room for it by expanding their idea of the natural order in ways which will seem suspect to many scientists, no less than to many traditionalists.

For the separation of 'two cultures' against which Lord Snow (1959, 1963) inveighed is partly due to science itself. It reflects the

dualism which Descartes formalized when he separated the realm
of the human spirit from the physical realm which includes
l'homme machine. It is inevitable that science, as it turns its attention to men and societies, should fall foul of this dichotomy and
should feel the need to replace it by a hierarchy of domains, each
of which is distinguished by forms of organization not accessible
to levels below, though each remains conditioned by those which
operate at lower levels also.

In restoring the ancient concept of an hierarchic natural order,
communication science may play, I think, an important, if
unconscious, part. 'I believe that the conceptual separation of
information processes from energy processes, which has taken
place in the last two decades, will prove as important as the changes
in our concepts of matter and energy and of space and time, which
marked the earlier decades of the century. I believe that one
important effect of this innovation in our thinking will be to
deepen our understanding of social processes and especially of . . .
the normative process' (p. 159).

These are the thoughts developed in the last three papers.

The first of these pleads for the admission of 'appreciation' as a
form of 'behaviour', requiring study in its own right and accessible to analysis, if not to 'observation', especially in the deliberations of collective bodies.

The second explores more directly the part of human communication in the normative process.

The third examines the curious mutual relation between the
psycho-social sciences and the others. 'The subject-matter of
science includes men and societies. The psycho-social sciences
are thus one of several branches of science. . . . The whole of
science, on the other hand, is one among many forms of human
activity, all of which invite study by the psycho-social sciences'
(p. 176). Pursuit of the relations between these 'two Chinese boxes,
each of which claims to contain the other', leads to the conclusion
that 'the psycho-social sciences differ from the physical sciences in
the nature of their subject-matter, in the sources of their know-

ledge about it, and in their own relation to it. Such regularities as they can observe are inconstant artifacts of the system which they study and are affected by their studies. They lack sources of knowledge on which other sciences rely; they are enriched by knowledge of a kind which other sciences would hate to have; and they are deprived of distance which other sciences regard as essential. None the less, they formalize a body of tested knowledge and what they formalize is significant to other sciences and their own as the findings of other sciences can never be. For it alone provides the basis for an epistemology which can illuminate what they and all their scientific colleagues are doing and can hope to do and a critique essential to the effective working and intelligent use of humanity's most trusted instrument – science' (p. 206).

All but the first of these papers were written within the years 1963–7; exact dates are relevant at a time when appreciative systems are changing so fast. Most of them were written for special occasions; each has its own focus of interest and, I hope, its own coherence. But though they do not fit together like chapters of a book, I hope they will be found to lend each other the mutual support and clarification which this foreword claims for them.

I have not greatly modified them. The amount of repetition which I have allowed to remain in them may seem superfluous to those to whom the iterated view is clear from the first, but it will, I hope, be useful to others. For it is a central theme of the book that we learn to recognize new form, perceptual or conceptual, aesthetic, political, moral, or scientific, only by repeated and preferably willing exposure to it. I hope that these papers may help to naturalize in contemporary thought ways of appreciating our situation which seem to me useful, urgently needed, and impeded in their emergence by both our scientific and our humanist inheritance, though in truth they are heirs of both.

I have added to each paper a note describing the occasion which gave rise to it and acknowledging any publications in which it has appeared. I am grateful to the publishers and others who have concurred in my assembling them in book form; to those whose

invitations first evoked them; and to all whose responses to them
have helped my snail-like progress along the trail they mark.

II

With that I might leave the papers to speak for themselves. But I
have found such differences of view among friends and corres-
pondents, even in fields which I thought had long since ceased
to be controversial, that some further introductory comments
may be useful or interesting to some. I hope that others will skip
them or bear with them.

To readers who prize scientific knowledge for its supposed
independence of imprecise verbal expression, I would suggest the
possibility that three hundred years of scientific observation and
experiment may have led us to underrate the significance and power
of words.

Babies, including the greatest future scientists, are humanized,
as well as socialized, by being talked to and encouraged to talk.
Human communication claims them and equips them from birth
to function as members of a specific, communicating human group.
In doing so, it provides them with its own ways of thinking and
talking about experience. It introduces them to a conceptual world,
already culturally shaped, which is their human heritage. However much they may later criticize, reject, or reshape this heritage,
it is their only entry into human life. Given this in childhood,
they can later support much physical and psychological isolation.
Yet without this early, humanizing mediation of language and
culture, we have good reason to think that even the greatest
potential astronomer could not so much as notice a star.

Clearly, we must credit our kind with distinctive human
capacities which become actual only by being exercised in early
years by assimilation into an existing culture. We do not know
fully what these capacities are and it seems most unlikely that we
ever shall; for we have no means of exploring them, except the
capacities themselves, and it seems logically unlikely that any

creature could be so equipped as fully to understand itself. None the less, we know something about our specifically human selves; and we may hope to know more. The newest source of possible knowledge is the extension of science into the field of communication.

Students of human genius distinguish at least four general categories in which human 'giftedness' can be discerned – intellectual, inventive, aesthetic, and social. No one can live for long in any culture without noticing that he and his fellows differ widely in all these abilities and doubtless others. These differences in human excellence, however, are crossed and sometimes masked by cultural differences. How rational are we expected to be? What abstract ideas are we expected to entertain? How far are we expected to anticipate and respond to the future? How appreciative are we expected to be of significant form of various kinds? How sensitive to each other? In all such questions the governing expectations are inherent in the cultures and sub-cultures in which we participate; they mould, as well as assess, our development. They are many; a single family may have a distinctive sub-culture.

Thus human life is sustained culturally, no less than biologically, by what seems to be a highly precarious process. Each generation takes over, makes over, and passes on a heritage which consists basically in specific ways of appreciating and acting in its situation. Each generation is both socialized and humanized in the process. This heritage subsists at any point of time in the organization of countless individual minds, never wholly shared; yet it is a social artifact, dependent on communication both for its continuity and for its change, yet itself giving meaning to the communication on which it depends.

This mutually dependent development of language and culture is seen at its most effective and least conspicuous in a society which is stable, coherent, and isolated from other cultures. Here time has established close correspondence between the needs and concerns of the society and the shared, symbolic system by which these are represented and interpreted in language and thought. The symbolic system fits the 'facts of life' so comfortably that those who are born to it cannot distinguish the one from the other – however ill matched they may seem to a visiting anthropologist.

This shared symbolic system is itself one of the facts of life. To the visiting anthropologist it is as much a fact of the situation as climate or diet or endemic disease. It is, however, a fact of a different order and its difference lies in the process by which it is maintained and changed. This process is of critical importance and it is the main theme of this book. For it is essential to any society that its appreciative system shall change sufficiently to interpret a changing world, yet should remain sufficiently shared and sufficiently stable to mediate mutual understanding and common action and to make sense of personal experience. These demands manifestly conflict with each other increasingly as rates of change accelerate and contacts between disparate cultures multiply. This conflict seems to me to be the main characteristic of our time.

Clearly, it is of the first importance to any society to ensure the continuity through time and change of that appreciative system which is to human life what humus is to the planet. 'When the first seed-bearing plants began to release their seeds to the wind's distribution, no mind could have foretold, if mind had been there to speculate, that, rooting and dying on the infertile wastes, their own decay would build up a bed of humus in which unimagined successors would evolve and flourish. We are guardians of a social humus more precious and more vulnerable than theirs – guardians not merely of values but of the soil in which values grow. Conservators and innovators alike, our paramount duty to the future is to leave it a little deeper for our passage' (p. 69).

III

The imprecision of words, the 'openness' of their meanings, is essential to the growth of our appreciative system and provides the key to its ability to preserve continuity through change.

This is true even in the realm of physical science. The atomic theory guided men's thought about the architecture of matter – with uncanny precision – for two thousand years before the first observation or calculation supplied any evidence of its validity. Almost immediately, accumulating evidence showed that 'a-toms' lacked both the qualities with which they had been credited; they were neither indivisible nor indestructible. But the atomic theory was not discredited. Atomic physics burgeoned into a sub-atomic world, peopled by 'particles' which appear to lack that most basic character of particularity – identity.

Over the same period, the concept of democracy has influenced men's thought about the architecture of political society, in a curiously similar way, though the field is one in which their thought would seem to have a greater chance of shaping its subject-matter. Today at least two political theories (at daggers drawn) claim the name of democracy; each has several variants; and all are in rapid change. The thought invites us not to cynicism but to hope. Word-frozen creeds are history's nightmares.

The hope, however, needs qualification.

For a relatively brief but immensely important period in the history (largely) of Western Europe, emancipation was believed to be the necessary and sufficient condition of human 'progress'. '. . . to dethrone tyranny, to dispel superstition, and to clear the channels of trade were equally blows in the battle of emancipation' (p. 6). Freed from these impediments, human reason, working on accumulating knowledge, would provide a sure guide to the harmonious life of men on earth. 'Condorcet, waiting for the guillotine, looked forward, as to a millennium, to the day when the sun would shine on "an earth of none but free men with no master save reason"' (p. 7). The battle for emancipation still rages, with a ferocity powered partly by the cultural valuations generated in the last two centuries. But the man with no master save reason has gone with the noble savage into the limbo of unmasked self-contradictions. Human freedom, like every other desired human condition, can only be part of the dowry of some

xix

specific culture; and reason, however conceived, can contribute to freedom only by shaping that culture. And even this it cannot do unless it is conceived in terms more congenial to St Thomas Aquinas than to the Rand Corporation (p. 95). For the main choices which it has to guide are those multi-valued, political choices which express current priorities among a society's aspirations. The papers in the second part attempt to show how inadequate is our contemporary idea of 'reason' to explain both what we attempt and what we achieve in this basic political task.

Our idea of reason may prove to be as open to revision as our idea of time has recently been found to be.

In so far as these papers express my belief in a 'post-Cartesian' world, neither dualistic nor monistic but hierarchic, I shall probably be rated by some as 'unscientific'. In so far as they attribute high significance to communication science and its neo-mechanical models of mental process, I shall surely be regarded by others as 'reductionist'. It may be useful that I should add a few words to ensure so far as may be that such criticisms are directed to what I am actually saying.

Science has formulated the natural order in terms of physical laws applicable to all material things; biological laws applicable to all organic systems; psychological laws applicable (largely) to creatures with nervous systems; social and ecological laws applicable to human and non-human populations. All these laws apply equally to our own kind; without them we could not begin to understand or handle our current predicament – nor should we have had the means to create it. But the concept of the natural order which science has thus formulated is too narrow to account for science or scientists or their fellow-men. Anyone wishing to think about human affairs, whether scientifically or non-scientifically, must in practice, I think, admit the existence of a further and specifically human domain, obedient to all these laws and conditioned by them but not fully explained by them, since its very existence testifies to the emergence of yet another field or principle of organization. This domain is the conceptual, value-structured world which is embodied in and transmitted by human cultures and which has been made possible by human communication.

This view of the natural order presents it not as dualistic, as Descartes saw it, nor as monistic, as it appeared to nineteenth-century 'materialists' and still appears to many today; but as a hierarchy – an ancient concept which in its modern form may be capable of unifying our understanding of the natural order; enlarging it sufficiently to contain ourselves; and defining the logical limits of our own comprehension of it. This achievement would not only resolve some of the problems and pseudo-problems of philosophy. It would also resolve or at least define some of the practical problems which beset the methods and the evaluations of the psycho-social sciences.

Current developments in communication science are not, I think, necessary to support this view[1] nor are they currently conceived as doing so. None the less, they will, I think, have profound and useful effects on our ideas of reality, as well as of communication.

They will lead us to attach due importance to the difference between systems which are open only to the exchange of matter and energy and those which are also open to the exchange of information, a distinction for which we have at present not even a name. A space satellite, a system open to information as well as energy, is clearly not to be fully explained in terms of the principles governing simpler machines which are open to exchanges of energy alone, although, of course, they are equally obedient to those principles. Personal and social systems can be shown, I think, to exemplify still higher levels of organization.

Again, communication science already provides us with an analogy to the relation of brain and mind which, however crude,

[1] Professor Polanyi has argued persuasively that even the simplest machine is not explicable in terms of physics and chemistry alone. These may account for a breakdown; but the criteria of 'going right' and 'going wrong', essential to the concept of a machine, derive from operational principles unknown to physics and chemistry.

is better than we have had at our disposal until now. Brains may prove to operate in some ways which are radically different from those of any computer we now possess or conceive. I think they will (p. 104). They are certainly 'programmed' by experience in ways remote from those in which any man-made computer is, or perhaps could be, programmed. It remains immensely useful that we should have learned even the elementary lesson that a computer and its programme are different kinds of entity, though a computer is only potentially a computer until it is programmed. Such distinctions, obvious as they are, were unknown a few decades ago. They should serve to still some of the silliest confusions between brain and mind and should leave the word 'material' an embarrassment until it has been purged of its nineteenth-century overtones.

I do not at present share the more optimistic hopes of those who try to simulate mental processes on machines; but I believe that their efforts, however well or badly they succeed, will equally help to establish human 'appreciation' as a distinctive and accept-able feature of the natural order and to establish the status and character of its most important and unique creation – this shared, yet inner world of terror and delight, this hall of mutually reflect-ing and distorting mirrors, in which, among other queer and fragmentary appearances, we seem sometimes to see – ourselves.

REFERENCES

SNOW, C. P. 1959. *The Two Cultures*. London: Cambridge University Press.
SNOW, C. P. 1963. *A Second Look*. London: Cambridge University Press.
SNOW, C. P. 1964. *The Two Cultures and a Second Look*. London: Cambridge University Press; New York: New American Library.

Part One

The Ecology of Ideas

Some Ideas of Progress

The belief in Progress, in its short life, has embraced several mutually inconsistent ideas; it is hard to find any which is shared by every version of the faith. All, however, seem to me to proceed from one common assumption, which might be called the 'faith in Process'.

According to this view, the stream of events which forms the substance of history is neither a random sequence nor a providential plan but is the result of process. Men, all organisms, all matter indeed, interact in accordance with laws which are imperfectly known but which are believed to be discoverable and assumed to be constant. Today is for ever giving birth to tomorrow and tomorrow will necessarily be different; for change is inherent in the process. Now in some respects – and here is a crucial aspect of the faith – the direction of this change is and will be both constant and welcome. Such change, which is not self-limiting or circular but linear, if it is expected to be at least acceptable, is called Progress.

The mainspring of Progress is the accumulation of knowledge. Since, in Bacon's words, 'the inescapable propriety of Time is ever more and more to disclose Truth', each generation is bound to see more deeply than its predecessors into the nature of the process of which it is part. Whatever may be the effect of this increasing knowledge, it is likely, by and large, to be constant in its direction and to produce progressively 'better' conditions for men on earth.

Four major issues have always divided the votaries of Progress. What is the nature of the process ? How does increasing knowledge cause men to act upon it ? In what fields does it produce the kind of change called progress? In what sense is this progress good? To all these questions divergent answers have been returned. Some have found the key to the process in competition between individuals, some in conflict between classes, some in co-operation within and between groups. Some have supposed that enlightened man could do no more than co-operate with a process which he could neither reverse nor control; others have believed that he could and would increasingly shape his own destiny. Some have thought of Progress only as multiplying goods or elaborating organization; others have found it in politics, in social relations, even in religion and Art. Some have found the criterion of good in 'happiness', others in 'right'. In trying to sort out this tangle of ideas, my chief concern will be to ask what kind of process each implies and how well this agrees with what little we do know about the process of which we are part. Our faith in progress, if we hold one, may soar beyond the evidence, but our idea of progress must be grounded in our understanding of the process from which alone it can proceed.

II

The ancient world was not without the idea of 'Process'; but with curious unanimity it assumed that the world process was one of cyclical degeneration. It knew well enough that the useful arts had increased and might increase still further. Lucretius speaks of men 'progressing step by step' from their early savage state, and St Augustine describes the progress of technology in language which would not have been out of place today; yet for Lucretius this progress is only an incident in a far-spent decline from a golden age, while St Augustine recites the technical triumphs of his time only to distinguish the arts which adorn life on earth from the virtues which lead to bliss in heaven. Atheist and Christian, at odds about so much, are united at least in this. Neither sees material progress as evidence of success in a method which will in time reveal the secrets of life. Neither conceives as possible or desirable a material world ordered by man for his ease and convenience. Neither, indeed, has any hope in history.

In this they are not alone, Baillie (1950), surveying ancient civilizations, writes: 'What is to us most remarkable about the mentality of all those pagan cultures is the absence ... of anything like *hope*.' In some there was indeed hope of release, even of reward, for the individual soul; but in only two ancient religions does he find any hope in history. Of these Judaism was already projecting its Messianic hope beyond the field of history when Christianity was born; and Christian doctrine, though it assigned a meaning to history, did not encourage men to pin their hopes on the redemption of human society on earth.

The most famous account in English of a 'Progress' was written by John Bunyan: but the progress of his pilgrim is as remote as could be imagined from the kind of progress which was to inspire Christians as well as worldlings two hundred years later. His progress was a purely individual affair. It aimed at a goal which must be wholly attained or wholly missed. It did not substantially ease the path of future pilgrims. The world through which he progressed was a snare and a delusion. He owed it no duty and it offered him nothing but the prospect of damnation. It is indeed a far cry from Vanity Fair to the Welfare State.

Dean Inge (1920), in a well-known lecture on this subject, points out that this picture of the ancient world is somewhat overdrawn. They too knew their great ages, even their ages of complacency; but even at their most assured they did not conceive these phases of 'progress' as the product of a process which was set to roll onwards indefinitely, still less as the opening of a time in which man would be increasingly master of his destiny. Man, even at his greatest, seemed a Promethean figure; the hopes of the age of Palmerston would have shocked the age of Pericles even more than some of its achievements.

Something happened in the two centuries between, say, 1550 and 1750 to attune the mind of Western man to an idea which was fundamentally new – the idea that time might not be an enemy but an ally, that change might be the expression of a trend upwards. Bury (1920) has traced this preparatory stage as a phase in the history of thought, describing the decay of those classical and Christian concepts which stood in the way of the new values, the corresponding growth of confidence in the familiar earth as an adequate field for the future blessedness of mankind and in man's science as an instrument for bringing it to pass. Others have described the same period as a phase of economic and of social history. The confidence of that time moulded expectations in many fields. I choose two. Men conceived the ideas of political progress and of economic progress and each idea became the core of a faith.

III

These two ideas seem to me radically different. Political progress is continuous change in the direction of 'better' government (whatever that may be taken to mean); economic progress is continuous change in the direction of 'more wealth' for 'less' effort. Thus, the two goals are not comparable; progress towards them is not measurable in similar terms. So we cannot assume that one process accounts for the two or even that they are fully compatible. To mark the difference, whatever it may be, I shall usually refer to economic progress as 'expansion' and to political progress as 'betterment'. It has proved, I think, no small misfortune that the idea of economic expansion and the idea of political betterment got loose in the world at the same time.

Their disparities were not so apparent in the eighteenth century. Political change and economic growth were both facts of experience but they seemed to be facts of the same sort and they elicited the same response. Emancipation was the gospel of the day; to dethrone tyranny, to dispel superstition, and to clear the channels of trade were equally blows in the battle of emancipation. Few who fought in the faith of freedom had deduced it from any clear idea about the process which liberty would unchain; yet increasingly during the years which closed the eighteenth and opened the nineteenth century men were thinking about the underlying process from which progress was to proceed and they were reaching two very different views, which maintain their rivalry even today.

It was generally assumed that the behaviour of men and societies was regulated by laws no less constant and no less discoverable than those which governed the solar system. Kant said that a Kepler or a Newton was needed to find the law of the movement of civilization, and in the eighteenth century men were searching for the law as assiduously and much more optimistically than we are today. Meantime, they assumed that it existed and they expected of it more than they expected from the laws of the solar system; for those laws, so far as was then known, did not initiate any progressive change but merely maintained balance. Civilization, on the other hand, was obviously on the march. What laws must govern the interaction of men with each other and with the physical environment, if the resultant progress was that which historians noted and political prophets foretold?

According to one view, the only law which need be postulated was the human being's tendency to seek its own interest and the human capacity through reason to see where its interest lay. The interaction of increasingly enlightened and constantly self-seeking men would result both in political and in economic progress. Condorcet, waiting for the guillotine, looked forward, as to a millennium, to the day when the sun would shine on 'an earth of none but free men with no master save reason', never doubting that reasonable men would see where their interest lay and that free men would follow where reason pointed. The faith assumed that men's interests were constant and were not fundamentally inconsistent and were ascertainable by reason and that the pursuit of them would not be self-defeating. Man's conscious part was not to guide the process, which was neither possible nor necessary, but to create the conditions for its free functioning.

7

Liberty was the condition and self-interest the driving force of the process and increasing happiness would be its product.

This was a genuine theory of progress, in that it claimed to describe a process which would yield welcome change in a constant direction. Its shortcomings are well known; it failed to take account of the sociality of human life; its theory of human motivation was grossly inadequate. These defects, however, were less fatal to it as an analysis of economic than of political progress. It was possible to show that individual men pursuing their own economic interests might through the market satisfy each other's needs; that more division of labour, expanding markets, and growing trade were three mutually exciting factors, which, if free to operate, would increase the wealth of nations without any obvious limit.

On the political side, the analysis was much less satisfactory. The process by which free interaction would produce better government was never postulated so clearly as the process by which it would produce more wealth. The conditions in which individual wills would merge in a general will were never so clear as the conditions in which individual demands would satisfy each other. The political man was a much less predictable animal than the economic man – and he still is. We can say why we had a depression in 1931 much more confidently than we can say why we had wars in 1914 and 1939.

The other view was fundamentally different. It took a multitude of political forms, but all made a common assumption about the process. Progress was to be expected because men were perfectible and they were perfectible because they were plastic. Human institutions were the means by which they were to be moulded. The underlying process worked by progressively shaping human institutions.

These views were the heirs of a long tradition. The earlier world expected betterment only from good laws; certainly not from blind or selfish interaction. Philosophers from Plato onwards had based their Utopias on the wisdom of a lawgiver. To

8

them, however, the problem had been how to protect the structure, once created, from decay. It was left to the age of hope to
conceive of a *progressive* course of education and legislation,
leading through even better institutions to an ever-improving
polity.

This sort of progress could not be explained as the result of a
process driven and guided solely by individual self-interest,
however enlightened. Selfish men might satisfy one another in the
market-place but why should they combine to pursue remote ends
for the benefit of posterity? How indeed could they be expected to
agree upon such ends? And why should these ends remain constant? These questions needed an answer from those who claimed
to have a reasoned hope that men could and would perfect themselves; but the then current psychology could not begin to answer
any of them. It could not even show why men should identify
their own happiness, however defined, with that of the 'greatest
number', especially when it is acknowledged that the greatest
number are the unborn. Thus even the strictest Utilitarian creed,
once it aspired to be more than an economic analysis, had to admit
values which it could not justify. Political betterment, in fact, is an
inescapably ethical idea, though economic expansion need not be;
for it is impossible to formulate the idea of a process leading to
political progress without introducing in some form the idea of a
good which can be progressively realized and of a duty owed both
to neighbour and to posterity to work for its realization.

The idea of betterment, like the idea of expansion, may be
associated with very different ideas of process. On the one hand
the process may be thought of as working independently of human
guidance through the growing enlightenment of individual men;
on the other hand it may be held that men will increasingly come
to direct it and indeed that progress is the result of this increasing
element of self-direction. In short, it may be thought of either as a
kind of evolution or as a branch of social engineering. The
difference may be fundamental in many ways; but all theories of
progress, however much they may differ in this respect, must

9

imply a process which has a direction and therefore which can find constant criteria by which direction can be measured.

They are therefore opposed to theories of process which regard change as *mere* adjustment, since such theories offer no prospect of change in any constant direction except adaptability. Yet every theory of process must find room for changes of this kind. They are indeed the only clear and universal kinds of change, and they are bound to be oscillatory. Some have found in the tendency of action to provoke reaction the key to history. Inge, in another essay, says: 'Every institution not only carries with it the seeds of its own dissolution but prepares the way for its most hated rival.'

These oscillations seem like balancing movements and any adequate theory of process must explain them.

Balance, expansion, betterment – these three ideas are different in character yet interrelated. The faith in progress must assert that the process of history operates in all these three dimensions; that it achieves or at least will achieve not only stability but expansion; not only expansion but betterment; and those who hold it are challenged to produce an analysis of the process showing how this can occur. No such analysis has yet appeared; but faiths, even when well founded, usually precede any clear understanding of the facts which support them.

IV

The faith in Progress which was to rule England for a century simplified its problem by identifying expansion with betterment and ignoring balance altogether – a feat of mental occlusion which would only have been possible in the early stages of an expansionist age. This form of the faith was thus expressed by a French economist, Mercier de la Rivière, in about 1760: 'Humanly speaking the greatest happiness possible for us consists in the greatest possible abundance of objects suitable for our enjoyment and in the greatest liberty to profit by them.'

The twin goals of Progress, as it was to be conceived in England for the next hundred years, could not be more clearly or indeed more crudely described; and here is how it looked to a contemporary Englishman, Joseph Priestley:

'... nature, including both its materials and its laws, will be more at our command, men will make their situation in this world abundantly more easy and comfortable, they will probably prolong their existence in it and will grow daily more happy ... thus, whatever was the beginning of the world, the end will be glorious and paradisiacal beyond what our imaginations can now conceive. Extravagant as some people may suppose these views to be, I think I could show them to be fairly suggested by the true theory of human nature and to arise from the natural course of human affairs.'

Progress is conceived as proceeding automatically from human nature and from 'the natural course of human affairs'. Its direction is constant, its course indefinite and its results 'paradisiacal'. The wealth of nations is indefinitely expansible by the division of human labour, internationally we well as nationally. This great principle is to be realized through free competition, which automatically makes for the most efficient division of labour. It will eliminate frontiers (which are deemed to be artificial) and wars (which are deemed to be irrational and therefore unnecessary) and will unite the world in the Great Commercial Republic. So clear the way for the great, natural principle, whereby each benefits his neighbours by enriching himself! Ring out division, limitation, tradition! Ring in the Great Commercial Republic and the Parliament of Man!

There is no doubt that the men of that and the succeeding generation believed that they had stumbled on a truth of universal application and incalculable power. In 1851 the Prince Consort, opening the Great Exhibition, said:

'Nobody who has paid any attention to the peculiar features of our present era will doubt for a moment that we are living in a period of most wonderful transition, which tends rapidly to accomplish that great end to which all history points – the realization of the unity of mankind.'

The age which saw so fantastic an increase in 'the abundance of objects suitable for our enjoyment' may seem in retrospect material. Quotations such as this – and they could be multiplied indefinitely – show that this would be a shallow judgement. I believe that no such faith had animated these islands since the days when the cathedrals were built, that no vision of last things had so powerfully possessed men's imaginations since they ceased to expect the Second Coming.

In the middle of the century Karl Marx announced what seemed a startlingly new theory of Progress, in that he denied the identity of interests which the Utilitarians had assumed and asserted instead a divergence of interest so sharp that it could only be resolved by conflict. The process consisted in the development of this divergence, in the resultant class war, and in its inevitable outcome. Here again was a process with which men could co-operate by sharpening the issues and precipitating the conflict. Thereafter the process would take a different course. Since the victory of the proletariat would have removed the cause for the exploitation of persons, history thereafter would be the uneventful, co-operative administration of things.

The thoughts of Karl Marx became the core of a fighting faith which today numbers far more adherents than any other; and it also affected the idea of Progress even in the minds of its opponents. It stressed the part played by conflict in the process and incidentally also the part played by co-operation – two forms of interaction which are, I think, distinct from competition. It challenged all value judgements to show their credentials and cast on those who maintained them the burden of proving that they were not mere rationalizations of self-interest. It introduced new ideas about the working of the economic process, ideas which may become still more important in the future, since most of the world's economic expansion during the next chapter of history seems likely to take place among peoples now dominated by marxist ideas.

Yet its underlying concepts were in some ways curiously like those of the classical economists. By denying what they affirmed and attacking as the root of all evil that use of private property which was the cornerstone of their system, Marx turned their world upside down, but it was the same world. His thoughts may have speeded but did not cause the changes which have filled the century since his day and which set problems which are common to communist and non-communist countries today.

From the last quarter of the nineteenth century Progress in England was beginning to disappoint men's hopes in several ways. It distributed its fruits in a way which became increasingly unacceptable to the many; it developed ever-increasing oscillations between boom and slump; and it played increasing havoc both with the physical and with the social environment. This shook men's faith in the simple conception of process as the interaction of individual self-interest.

It appeared that emancipation was not enough. It was not enough to let the process run free; its results must be controlled at least as regards the distribution of the spoil.

Further, it appeared that expansion was not enough. Stability took its place beside expansion as a goal of progress – not an antithesis, nor merely as a limiting condition, but as a good in its own right.

Finally it appeared that expansion might be self-defeating, not only through its own deficiencies but even through its own success. Individual liberty included liberty to combine; yet, when so used, it seemed to fetter itself. Competition eliminated the unfit; yet, pushed to the limit, it left the fittest with a monopoly. The tendency of all movements to breed their own limitations was becoming too apparent to be ignored.

During the next hundred years our idea of process underwent a deep and subtle change and our corresponding idea of Progress was chastened but not extinguished; indeed it has in some degree been amplified. This change has not had its prophet; no Bentham or Marx has arisen to proclaim it as a new gospel. And though from time to time politicians and political scientists have explicitly revised their theories, they have done so in order to square them with new lines of policy which were already emerging as inescapable responses to the situation.

Thus in 1902 the late Lord Samuel (Samuel, 1902), then a young Liberal politician, wrote a book to explain why the party, when it came to power, was to adopt a policy of social legislation which seemed deeply at variance with the philosophy of *laissez-faire*. The book is a vivid reminder of what the social problem meant at the turn of the century, with what anxiety new weapons were forged to meet it – and, incidentally, how effective those weapons have been.

The new weapons were, indeed, not new. They had been coming into use in England for fifty years. Dicey (1905) dates the beginning of 'socialist' legislation in England in 1856. (Significantly the occasion was the first refusal of Parliament to pass a bill for enclosing a common.) The stream flowed ever more freely until 1906, when the new Liberal administration began to implement the policies described in Lord Samuel's book. From then until now the volume has increased, the flow has quickened. Though often the focus of party strife, the trend has not been the work of any single political party. Differences of principle have masked striking similarities of practice.

One characteristic of the period has been the need to produce more collective responses and the progressive integration of the groups from which these responses were required. Central and local governments and trade unions, all grew stronger. Businesses grew and federated in associations. We can summarize the change as the progressive integration of groups, in which each individual's responses are increasingly conditioned by the organized relations of his group.

If we look for implications of a change in the conception of process, we can see waning the idea of progress through the interaction of competing self-interest and ascendant the idea of progress as the expression of a social purpose, which comprehends economic as well as political goals and more beside; for the economic man and the political man have begun to merge in a new concept, less remote from human nature – the social man, whose well-being is now the criterion of progress. More and more we think of the process as dependent on conscious, collective control.

If we seek a measure of this new progress we can no longer answer blandly 'happiness', for the days are gone when political philosophers talked of happiness as if it were a commodity to be weighed like butter in a grocer's scales. Yet, however naïve the idea may seem, an important part of it still persists, thinly disguised as 'the standard of living'. Whatever else progress may have come to mean, it still means for nearly all of us that collectively at least we should go on consuming progressively more and more – an idea which may prove to be a cuckoo in our intellectual nest. Though expansion and betterment, once identified, are seen as distinct, expansion remains linked to betterment as an indispensable pre-condition.

If we ask what is the process from which this social purpose proceeds, we are in the difficulty which beset the eighteenth century. This is due partly to our ignorance of the basic process. How profoundly our assumptions have changed can be judged by comparing the 'new' Poor Law of 1834 with our present system of National Assistance as established in 1948. The architects of the Poor Law of 1834 had no doubt that they understood the process and that the institutions which they were fashioning in the light of that understanding would abolish destitution within a generation. In just over a century the last traces of their work were swept away and all parties joined in repudiating their principles; yet our new idea of the process, though clear in what it repudiates, is by no means so assured in what it asserts. The laws of human interaction are still obscure.

Moreover, apart from this basic ignorance, we see more clearly the difficulty of formulating any theory of progress. This is partly because of the emergent inconsistency between expansion and betterment and partly because of the tendency of any movement in either dimension to breed its own limitations. If expansion and betterment are not necessarily compatible with each other, the demands of 'balance' seem inconsistent with both.

At this point it is useful to seek enlightenment on the ideas of progress and process in other fields.

V

Biologists have tried and discarded many definitions of biological progress. Julian Huxley (1954) writes:

'There have been many attempts to define biological progress or advance in organisation. It would seem that the most satisfactory definition is as follows. Biological progress consists in biological improvements which permit or facilitate further improvements. Such *non-restrictive improvement* constitutes a very special and very important category of evolutionary progress and assuredly merits a special name. It is a rare phenomenon. Most evolutionary trends come to an end ... by the Pliocene only one path of progress remained open – that which led to man. The last step of progress was a continuance of the trend towards increased awareness ... Once the critical point was passed at which conceptual thought and true speech could develop, a new method of evolution became possible – the method of cultural transformation, based upon the cumulative transmission of experience ... The new phase of evolution ... was characterised by a new relation between the organism and its environment. The human type became a microcosm which through its capacities for awareness was able to incorporate increasing amounts of the macrocosm into itself, to organise them in new and richer ways and then through their aid to exert new and more powerful influences on the macrocosm. And the present situation represents a further highly remarkable point in the development of our planet, the critical point at which the evolutionary process ... has for the first time become aware of itself ... evolution is on the verge of becoming internalised, conscious and self-directing.'

This definition depends in turn on the meaning of 'improvement' which Professor Huxley defines as 'any increase in the efficiency of living organisms regarded as machines for carrying on the business of living and reproducing themselves in the environment provided by this planet'.

This passage is, I think, important in several ways. First, it asserts that the only progress which can be expected from the process of biological evolution is progress in adaptability; and even this is not achieved by accumulating experience, but simply by progressively eliminating all but those best equipped to adapt. Next, it asserts that the process has given birth to another which runs concurrently but is not of the same kind, namely the process by which experience is transmitted. Finally, it asserts that the process has reached a stage at which it is about to become self-directing. If this is so, it remains to ask whither and by what criteria. Is it to direct itself merely towards more refined adjustments? Or is it developing goals of its own?

On this point Sir Julian Huxley's grandfather, Dr T. H. Huxley (1894), had no doubts at all. In a famous lecture in 1893 he said:

'... the evolution of society is, in fact, a process of an essentially different character ... from that which brings about the evolution of species...'

and again:

'Social progress means the checking of the cosmic process at every step and the substitution for it of another which may be called the ethical process.'

Further:

'That which lies before the human race is a constant struggle to maintain and improve, in opposition to the state of Nature, the state of Art of an organised polity; in which and by which men may develop a worthy civilisation capable of maintaining and constantly improving itself...'

To temper optimism he added:

'Until the evolution of our globe shall have entered so far upon its downward course that the cosmic process resumes its sway ... Evolution encourages no millennial expectations.'

While it would be unfair to quote his words without this rider, I do not feel that it is material. In the very long run we may all accept that man and his works will vanish and leave no trace; yet

17

it still remains valid to ask whether the probably very great span of time which still lies before us will see any form of progress or only the ebb and flow of a tide.

Huxley does not define the process which is to produce this ethical evolution. It remains to ask – 'Whence comes the initiative for this "struggle to maintain and improve ... the state of Art of an organised polity ..." to "develop a worthy civilization capable of maintaining and constantly improving itself ...".' Man is not God, to stand above the process and direct it. He is part of the process and no account of process is adequate which does not account for his initiatives. If he is to impose progressively a 'state of Art', it must be by virtue of something constant in his nature – by virtue, indeed, of those ethical values from which the belief in progress can never escape for long.

In this century science has begun to cast a little light on human nature. We still know less about the behaviour of men and nations than we do about the behaviour of atoms and nebulae, but at least we know more than our grandfathers did and we can see the new knowledge at work everywhere around us – in the running of social services such as education, health, and welfare; in the treatment of mental illness and crime; most of all, perhaps, in the re-making of human relationships within the authoritarian structure of business. I count it no small thing that psychiatry should recognize the power of love to make whole and keep whole the personality of man – even though the same truth was stated more clearly and comprehensively some twenty centuries ago. I find it striking to reflect how deeply within the last few decades ordinary men have absorbed the idea that fear and insecurity are root evils, that stable relationships and hence secure mutual expectations between man and man are fundamental conditions of well-being. Some would hold that truths like these give us for the first time a reasoned hope of progress in the dimension of human betterment; for enlightenment has begun to tell us what we most need to know. We are beginning to collect a few agreed notions about what are the really important conditions for living.

We are also on our guard against regarding the human being either as an individual who can be considered in isolation from his social relations or at the other extreme as a cell in an organism. We still lack any adequate set of ideas – or indeed of words – wherewith to deal with social phenomena, neither abstracting individuals nor personifying institutions; but we are approaching a better understanding of the process of human interaction.

VI

The idea of balance has been made much clearer by the study of ecology. Thus whenever we can examine the interaction of creatures with each other in an environment which is fairly constant, we find that their numbers and their way of life are adjusted to each other and to the environment in a way which is self-balancing. Whenever one variable changes, it sets in motion other changes which tends to restore the previous position.

Sometimes the limits are set by factors outside the system, as when a bird population is limited by available nesting-sites; sometimes by factors produced by the system, as when a species not only limits another on which it preys, but is itself limited by the food supply which it thus controls. The delicate, mutual balances which exist in every such system have been much studied in recent years and periodically attract the notice of laymen, whenever some human interference with nature, such as an in-secticide, has unlooked-for repercussions.

These mutually adjusting systems exemplify dynamic balance. They have sought and found their own stability and, if they are disturbed, they will seek it and ultimately find it again. This power is not confined to systems of organic creatures. Self-stabilizing mechanisms, like the automatic controls of guns, show the same propensity; and the engineer's term 'feedback' has come into general use to describe the principle on which it works. Dr Ross Ashby (1952) has described the theory in completely general terms, analysing the meaning of stability and the conditions in which variables having the power to respond to each other will arrive at a state of balance and will preserve it by continuous mutual adjustment.

These ideas are beginning to provide us with a language and a set of mental images which make it easier for us to talk and think about progress. If we can picture the process of human interaction as a special case of something more general, we may find it easier to see in what it is peculiar.

The main peculiarities of human beings, considered as variables in a system, seem to me to be two; they have extraordinary and growing powers on the one hand to predict the future course of events and on the other hand to alter it. The first is the gift of science, the second of technology. Science teaches us the law and enables us to predict and to obey. Technology uses the law and enables us to alter and to exploit.

These two are clearly likely to have opposite effects. The first should make men the most adaptable of creatures; the second makes them the least ready to adapt, for, when they encounter a limitation, their tendency is not to adapt to it but to alter the limitation. For other creatures the natural environment is almost wholly constant or independently variable. Not so for man. He can affect it, as much as it can affect him; and he does so on an even larger scale, often on purpose and still more often by accident. He ventilates mines and irrigates deserts 'on purpose'. He pollutes the rivers and poisons the urban air 'by accident'.

This on its present scale is a recent characteristic of a small minority of the earth's inhabitants. I will call them 'Western man', though an increasing number of them are now in the East. There seems good reason to expect that the habit will become more general.

Clearly, a system containing creatures which deal with limitations in this way cannot attain stability as other systems attain it. Other creatures work out their dynamic balance within a framework of limitation; 'Western' men change the framework to suit themselves and they are proud of it. They believe that they have escaped from a stable into an expanding world. They need not adapt to their environment, so long as they can adapt their environment to themselves. Moreover some cherish the illusion that every conquest of the environment leaves less to be conquered in the future, that every increase in power is an increase in control. During two expanding centuries they have developed an implicit belief that the process is an expanding one which will always call for and always evoke a further exercise of human domination over the environment; and, with this metaphysical belief in the way things work, they have developed the corresponding ethic, that dominance over nature is the distinguishing mark of man, that to transcend a limitation is courageous and noble, to accept it is cowardly and base.

This may have been a natural, though I think it was a mistaken, view of man's relation with the physical environment in an expansionist age. It is certainly a disastrous guide to his relations with the social environment; and one result of expansion is that human beings form each other's environment and set each other's limitations to an even greater degree. The idea that liberty means freedom from limitation rather than freedom to choose our limitations is a particularly dangerous delusion for the overcrowded inhabitants of a rather small planet.

VII

For ultimately some limitations have to be accepted. The choice for our technological age is whether to accept 'natural' limitations or to impose upon itself 'artificial' ones – and our dilemma is that the ethic of emancipation rejects both.

The dilemma, however, must be faced in the end. Consider, for example, the growth of motoring in England. The early motor-car was limited by roads designed for wagons. We lifted the limitation by improving the roads; the motor-cars multiplied and caught up with the limitation. We cannot for ever expand roads fast enough to provide for all their potential users, if only because we cannot afford to submerge the whole island under tar macadam. So there must be limitations; the only question is whether they shall arise 'automatically' or be imposed 'deliberately'. The difference between the two is important and by no means simple.

If motor-cars increase and roads do not, motoring becomes even slower, more unpleasant, and more dangerous. More and more people find that motoring is not worth the money and use of motor-cars eventually stabilizes at a limit determined by the operation of many individual choices. This is what I have called automatic limitation.

Alternatively the machinery of collective choice may be invoked to avoid the waste and confusion of automatic limitation, by checking the growth of traffic at some earlier point. Now policy is involved. Shall we raise taxes and leave motoring to the rich? Or license cars in favour of the useful or the deserving? Or draw lots for them and favour the lucky? We may be unable to make a collective choice in favour of these or any other alternative, because we are so organized that we cannot respond to that sort of question; and if we have no means of saying a collective 'yes', then, however great the need, the answer will be a collective 'no' – and the process will run on until individual choices impose an unplanned limitation.

One way or another a limitation will ultimately be reached; and if, as in this example, the limitation resulting from individual choice is one which no individual would choose, the adaptive capacity of the system tends to evolve machinery for collective choice, which will make possible an adequate response to the particular situation, though at the cost of making some other response more difficult.

We tend to suppose that the range of choice which is open to us, individually and collectively, is much wider than it really is. In fact, like other systems, the units in a human society have only a limited number of responses and these can be evoked by only a limited number of situations. When we alter our organization, political, economic, or social, we are changing the possibilities of our effective responses. In future some situations will evoke a response which formerly would not have done so – and vice versa. For we cannot answer more than a few questions at a time. To succeed is to be able to answer the questions which for the time being matter most.

Thus even in the dimension of economic expansion, where progress once seemed most assured, the future looks far from 'paradisiacal'; indeed it looks dark and uncertain – not because technological development seems likely to dry up but because of the changes which its own development creates. Population may beat the increasing food supply; wasting materials may beat our increasing skill in exploitation. And if, as some believe, ever-improving technique will always keep ahead of these two tireless pursuers, the changes which it must generate in doing so may beat our social skills. Politically, the individual choice becomes ever more confined by the collective choice; the path between anarchy and tyranny seems to grow ever narrower; and internationally the unity of mankind progresses, if at all, in a fashion very different from that which the Prince Consort had in mind. Perhaps Bunyan was right after all; even the progress of individual pilgrims may seem a less discouraging spectacle than the march of civilization.

To me at least the outlook does not seem so devoid of hope.

The dangers inherent in economic expansion are, I think, real and urgent. In Britain we have begun to adjust both our minds and our institutions to the subtly self-limiting nature of the process but far more slowly than the process demands. In some countries the change moves even more slowly, either because the time is not ripe or because the way is barred by the entrenched creeds of the past. Thus the Indian statistician Mahalanobis, pondering what distribution of India's capital investment will most quickly increase the flow of consumer goods, observes that he need not concern himself with problems of stability, of fluctuating employment, of booms and slumps. These are the problems of a mature economy. For India they are dwarfed by the need to provide within a generation for a population which will have doubled and which is already underfed. In the United States of America on the other hand, where the annual consumption of materials per head now exceeds eighteen tons per annum, the Paley Committee (1952) prefaced their report with a creed – perhaps one of the most significant utterances of our time – in which they affirm with passionate conviction that the continuance of this trend is the necessary basis for the spiritual values inherent in their way of life. I cannot pause to speculate on the probable course of affairs in a world where needs, abilities, and beliefs are so different and so inappropriately related to each other.

On the other hand, it is possible to feel some modest hope of progress in the art of maintaining dynamic balance. Deeper insight into the nature of the process must, it would seem, lead to quicker and more sensitive response, though progress in this dimension will be of no avail, if destabilizing factors increase their unpredictable impact even faster. The unskilled skater is wholly absorbed in keeping upright, yet always in process of some violent deviation, the slave of a system of oscillations which he can neither escape nor control. The skilled skater, whose balancing movements are no less continuous, is barely conscious of them; instead he is wholly absorbed in the delicious activity of skating. It is then not an unworthy ambition or an impossible hope that man, in his tottering progress along the cosmic tight-rope, may in time escape from his oscillatory antics and learn to walk nearly upright.

This modest hope is, I think, unlikely to be realized, unless we can realize also the more ambitious one of progress in what I have called 'betterment', by which I mean the progressive establishment of that 'state of Art' which Huxley acclaimed and which, despite all our disappointments, is being sought more determinedly today than ever before.

We stand very much where those philosophers stood two centuries ago who believed that men were perfectible through their institutions, except that we are more expert than they in the techniques and less confident than they in the result. All our institutions – the family, the school, the trade union, the business enterprise, the State – are inevitably agents in the process of transmitting experience and so moulding and conditioning each new generation. This process is, indeed, as Julian Huxley said, in process of becoming self-directing. The crucial question is whether there are inherent in the process any constant criteria by which it can direct itself. We know that, if it can perfect, it can also corrupt. Is there any reason to suppose that it does one more readily than the other – or indeed that the terms have objective meaning? Can the process do anything but seek 'adjustment'? What decides whether it will lead us to T. H. Huxley's 'worthy civilization', to Aldous Huxley's 'Brave New World', or to Orwell's '1984'?

Our answer to this must depend on our attitude to that fundamental question of ethics from which the hope of progress can never be divorced. Shall we one day read, among the truths which time is to disclose, not merely the law of civilization as it has been and as it is but also the law which it must follow if men are to fulfil and not to frustrate each other? Those who believe that there is such a law – and equally for all of them, whether they believe it to be derived from God or to be inherent in human nature or in the unchanging logic of the situation – must answer further whether it serves only to guide the individual life or whether it will become a force within the process which will progressively transform it. Those who would still believe in progress must answer 'yes' to both questions. In doing so, they must let their faith outrun our present understanding of the process but they need not, as far as I can see, assume anything inconsistent with the little we do know. It does not seem unreasonable to me to hope that our strange species should *progressively* learn the things which belong to its peace.

Yet if I may close on what may seem a chilling note, I have no doubt that any progress to which we may look forward in the near future – or perhaps in any future – will be progress in the art of saying 'no'. All choices are in fact largely negative; for every 'yes' implies a thousand 'noes'. From the bundle of possi-bilities in the perambulator to the old man on his deathbed whose last choice has been made, life consists in progressively actualizing a tiny proportion of the unnumbered possibilities with which we are born. Nearly all must go unrealized in any event; the quality and coherence of life lies in deciding which and how many shall be brought to being. Adjustment, balance, is a condition of being but not its sole law. Tillich (1954) writes: 'To be just to yourself means to actualise as many potentialities as possible without losing oneself in disruption and chaos' – an idea which he applies also to societies. Expansion, betterment, and balance are dimensions familiar to us in individual as in social life and the discipline of living in these three dimensions is no novelty, even though socially we are fumbling novices in living on the scale of today.

I therefore profess a personal faith that increasing knowledge promises us at least some guidance in the restraint of increasing power; that we shall not always use our increasing awareness 'to incorporate increasing amounts of the macrocosm . . .' or even 'to exert new and more powerful influences on the macrocosm'. Dingle (1952) describes as 'a profoundly disquieting menace to our civilisation' those who hold, with Professor Bernal, that science is 'the means of obtaining practical mastery over nature by understanding her'. These ideas may be current today but they could hardly have occurred to eighteenth-century minds, to whom science meant the triumphs of astronomy, gloriously generalized by Newton's law; and they may seem equally strange to a later age, to which some future Kepler or Newton has revealed 'the law of the movement of civilization'. Such a reversal would illustrate the tendency of movements to generate their own restraints; but it would not less on that account deserve to be called 'Progress'.

This paper was given as the Wilde Memorial Lecture to the Man-chester Literary and Philosophical Society in 1954 and published in the Society's Memoirs and Proceedings, Session 1954–5.

REFERENCES

ASHBY, W. ROSS 1952. *Design for a Brain*. London: Chapman & Hall.

BAILLIE, J. 1950. *Belief in Progress*. Toronto: Oxford University Press.

BURY, J. B. 1920. *The Idea of Progress*. London: Macmillan.

DINGLE, H. 1952. Introductory Essay. *The Scientific Adventure*. London: Pitman.

DICEY, A. V. 1905. *Law and Opinion in England in the Nineteenth Century*. London: Macmillan.

HUXLEY, J. 1954. Essay in Huxley, Hardy, and Ford (eds.), *Evolution as a Process*. London: Allen & Unwin.

HUXLEY, T. H. 1893. Romanes Lecture. Evolution and Ethics, published with Prolegomena in Romanes Lectures Decennial Volumes, 1892–1900 Oxford: Clarendon Press, 1900

INGE, W. H. 1920. The Idea of Progress. Romanes Lecture. Oxford: Humphrey Milford. Reprinted in appendix to *Diary of a Dean*.

PALEY. 1952. *Resources for Freedom*, Vol. I. Report to the President of the USA by the Materials Policy Commission. Washington: US Government Printing Office.

SAMUEL, H. 1902. *Liberalism*. London: Grant Richards.

TILLICH, P. 1954. *Love, Power and Justice*. London: Oxford University Press.

· 2 ·

Ecology, Planning
and the American Dream

Here I sit in my rural, ecological niche, metabolizing a breakfast drawn from three continents, and quietly increasing the world's supply of carbon dioxide, which, as Dr Deevey[1] explains, may be, but probably is not, helping to thaw the polar ice. Across the valley, through the tops of beeches, wych-elms, poplars, well grown in a century, I see the crest of the chalk hill, which rose from shallow, warm lagoons some fifty million years ago and which has since mantled itself with humus – that tattered robe, inches deep, which life, dying, has laid over earth's barren nakedness and in which alone new life can root. No longer grazed by sheep or rabbits, it has lost also the fine flora which once found a congenial home in the close-cropped turf; and, being now protected from human 'development' by a public trust, it is swiftly reverting to the woodland from which it was cleared in medieval times. Between me and the hill, the Thames follows the course which it took when it broke through these hills after the last ice age; but it is hidden by the multitude of unfolding leaves which compose the slow dream of a single spring.

Along that hill runs a track where I often walk; an old track as human pathways go, for it has been trodden by men and beasts for four thousand years, perhaps far more. Over many miles of grass it leads to the great earth and stone circles of Avebury, where, early in the second millennium before Christ, my predecessors here – including, I may hope, a few linear ancestors –

[1] See note on p. 50.

28

hewed with their antler picks, out of the solid chalk, a ditch twenty feet deep and a mile in circuit to guard their holy place; and piled up an artificial hill three hundred feet high. When they paused in that massive toil to look about them, they saw a landscape different from today's only in a few ways which I know or can guess. The bird voices, the hill contours, the shapes of leaf and tree which are familiar to me were no less familiar to them.

But from what *inner* world those men looked out, what the hill and rampart meant to them, what they saw as meaningful and what escaped their eyes for lack of foothold in their minds, all this I cannot even guess. If I could revisit them, I would expect to find much of their inner world alien or inaccessible. This, however, is equally true, though probably in lesser degree, of the visitor who will stay with me next week. And of them, as of him, I shall at least be sure that, though the objects of their hopes and fears may be beyond my comprehension, their hoping and their fearing will be to them as mine is to me. This conviction is itself odd, for it is unproved and unprovable; yet society in any form we know or value would dissolve if it were not universally held.

My inner world, I can safely say, would be far more strange to them. For at this moment, rooted here in a village community of man, beast, grass, grain, tree, I am equally absorbed in the community of minds which produced the papers in this book – men of other professions on the other side of the world, few of whom I have ever met; men engaged with problems of North American urban ecology, some of which have no counterpart here; yet men whose concerns I share and whose fellowship means much to me in two critical ways.

First, I share with them the excitement of a search for meaning, for understanding of one major aspect of mankind's current predicament: an interest sharpened both by the allure of intellectual challenge and by the need for action, no less here than there. (I live, maybe, in Arcady; but London is less than fifty miles away; and this village has its 'amenity association' of anxious citizens, trying to guide, if not to check, the tide of development which is submerging farm and garden and which will flood far more strongly when the projected motorway follows the neolithic track across the hills.)

Secondly, in my incommunicable inner world, I am upheld by the experience of this sharing, of making mine the thoughts of others, and of recognizing from their signals that my signals to them have been received.

These thoughts epitomize the main conceptual framework which these papers have left in my mind.

'Out there' is a 'real' world, in which things happen. To be more exact, it is a world of happenings, of relations and inter-actions: for even a stone in the mud or a brick in the wall may be thought of as an event in time – internally, as a configuration of forces; externally, as one constituent in a set of dynamic relations with its surround. Such a world is, naturally, a world of change; but also a world of stabilities and regularities, reflecting the regularities of its underlying laws. Science offers us at least two ways of thinking about these happenings. If we want to know what science can tell us about the way plants grow, we ask the botanist. If, on the other hand, we want to know why this hill, which fifty years ago was covered with vegetation an inch high, bears rank grass today and will be woodland in a few decades, we ask the ecologist. He will describe the effect on each other of the life cycles of the various denizens of these slopes, from the sheep to the tiniest grasses, and the effect on all of withdrawing one. The sheep and the rabbits kept down whatever plant growth could not renew itself from buds at ground level. The fine herbage flourished under their grazing, while the saplings perished. With-out sheep or rabbits, the balance was reversed. If pressed to explain the disappearance of the sheep and the rabbits, he would have to widen his field from the hillside to the planet and to take note of a greater variety of interacting forces. His answer, if he tried to make it complete, would take us through the economics of British farming, the response of Australian farmers to a plague of rabbits and of half-urbanized Britons to 'urban sprawl', and much else besides – again, the interaction of disparate variables within a single field.

This is the point of view of the ecologist, and of these papers; and the scene before me serves to illustrate its growing complexity. Before life colonized these hills, the physical forces at play there had established their mutual relationships, sometimes self-stabilizing and sometimes not. The great cycle of evaporation and precipitation maintained the planet's water supply in roughly constant balance between the sea, the atmosphere, the land surface, the subsoil, and the deep reservoirs; and the water, in its unceasing circuit, slowly eroded the newly risen hills and carved ever more deeply each gully which it had begun to carve before. On so recent an outcrop, however, the colonizing forces of life would have been soon at work. The seeding plants and grasses were ready to occupy the bare slopes, checking the erosion, deepening the humus in which they rooted, and modifying even the rainfall on which they subsisted. Skip half a million centuries and we are in a familiar world, in which the conspicuous forces in the ecological balance are forces of life, a fully developed threefold hierarchy, through which solar energy and minerals pass into plant form, thence to form and sustain the herbivores, thence to the carnivores and back again, with countless elaborations and short circuits.

Already the ecological balance is being maintained by forms of interaction which were unknown before the scene was animated. Each of these creatures, even the lowliest, can organize matter and energy into new and improbable patterns. Each can for a time preserve stable relations between its transient constituents by new methods of regulation; and each, equally, has new ways of regulating the relations between itself and its milieu, and hence new forms of interaction. In particular, most of these forms, even very lowly ones, can learn. There has been a progressive widening in the *field* of relevant interaction, in the *forces* operating within that field, and in the *kinds of interaction* involved.

Then comes the promise, and threat, of a far greater complexity.

The track runs across the hill crests to Avebury; the rampart is rising; the men who are moving those millions of tons of earth with muscles and wicker baskets are being fed by the labours of other men who must feed themselves as well. What new forces, interacting in what new field, are setting here their strange, enduring signature?

To understand Avebury, we should need to understand the social and technological organization of these neolithic men, which made possible this vast construction; and also their political and religious ideas, which caused it to take this form. To explain this development, we must admit the existence of a new field, unique within each head yet partly shared, an ill-defined but inescapable 'mental' field, which I have called their inner world: a world in which life can be not only lived but experienced and thought about, in which actual and hypothetical, past and future, can be equally present. The forces which operate in this new field, hope, fear, love, hate, ambition, loneliness, obligation, wonder, if not new, are raised to a new power and mediate by new forms of interaction – not only human speech, but all the arts of human intercourse, of mutual support, influence, coercion, manipulation.

This inner world, in which men inescapably live, develops in intimate relationship with the physical world, yet according to its own laws and its own time-scale. Human history can be understood only as the interaction of the two worlds. The inner world has its own realities, its own dynamism – and its own ecology. Like the life forms of the physical world, the dreams of men spread and colonize their inner world, clash, excite, modify, and destroy each other, or preserve their stability by making strange accommodations with their rivals. The meaning of Avebury, and the reasons why it was built, are to be found not in the ecology of the physical world but in the separate, though so closely related, ecology of the inner world – a world which was old when Avebury was built and which has developed since then far more strongly than the ecology of the surrounding hills.

This is even more true of all the institutions with which these papers deal. Much of the paradox and perplexity which haunt them is due to this essential duality of the world in which we live. Consider in briefest outline the stages of ecological development which this glance has covered. When the first vegetation began to colonize that hill, it found no rivals. There was room, it seemed, for all. Similarly, when the first colonists settled in North America, there must equally have seemed room for all. Actually, in each case there was room not for all but only for the few, rare types which could strike root here and there in such a habitat. As the hillside became one settled home of vegetable and animal life – and equally, as North America became one settled home of human life – the variety of living forms increased; and so did the variety and power of the forces which they brought to bear upon each other, limiting, sometimes eliminating, what had earlier been 'successful' types. Increasingly, in both cases, these forces, whether mutually enabling or mutually limiting, were produced by the activities of similar kinds of life, coming, as they multiplied, into ever closer contact with each other. Even in a milieu without man, the result was an increasingly complex pattern of interaction which can be classified as conflict, competition, or co-operation. Trees in a wood mutually stimulated their propensity to climb and mutually inhibited their propensity to spread. Sheep and rabbits maintained for the downland grasses and creeping plants a habitat as 'artificial' as the rich man's gardeners provide for his 'alpines'. With the emergence of man, these interactions of conflict, competition, and co-operation became elaborated in ways new in scale and character.

Avebury *could* not have been built except by a society whose food-getting technology was good enough to free large numbers of its members for unproductive work, and whose social technology was good enough to permit elaborate division of labour. These were already achievements possible to human society alone. Yet these alone do not explain the result. Avebury *would* not have been built, even by such a society, unless the dreams of the decision-takers had taken that form and the total value system of the society had been sufficiently strong and stable to support the implications of that decision for decades. It was a strange dream for men who were little better equipped for digging than the foxes and badgers that shared their native hills. The lonely ring among the brooding hills reminds us that the quality of our dreams is neither masked nor redeemed by the quality of our technology.

And so, as Peter Marris would agree, do the products of the United States Federal Housing Renewal Scheme.

II

The ecologist, in his complex analysis, develops some ideas which are of the greatest importance in assessing the significance of these papers.

He develops first the idea of *interdependence*. In a field of variables so closely and mutually interrelated, any change anywhere will in some degree affect the whole. As fields widen and variables multiply, this insight threatens to make the whole ecological approach too difficult to be useful. Happily, the ecologist finds that some groups of variables can be usefully studied *for some purposes* as if they were isolated. These groups may be local, be the locality as wide as the Amazonian rain forest or as small as the world under a paving stone. Alternatively, their members may be scattered over the planet, be their constituents as numerous as the members of the Roman Catholic Church or as few as the authors of these papers. The developing importance of such non-local groups is a feature of human society, with its unique systems of communication for mediating mutual influence over physical and temporal distances. The individual constituent may be a member of many groups, local and non-local – as I feel myself to be. Whether local or non-local, what makes a group a valid and useful field of study is that the interactions which are the subject of the study are largely confined within the group field. The relevant forces which bear on the members of the group from outside (be they the tropical rains of the Amazon or the traffic problems of North American cities) may be regarded as conditions common to the group.

Next, the ecologist comes to recognize certain *recurring patterns* in his field of study. These are of four main kinds. Perhaps the most interesting, because the least obviously to be expected, is the steady state. In a world of flux, it is constancy, not change, that requires explanation; and the ecologist's world contains a number of patterns which preserve themselves over substantial periods of time with little apparent change. Populations, for example, like organisms, sometimes remain stable for long periods, by exchanging and renewing their transient constituents at a constant rate.

The ecologist also recognizes change, in the form of increase or decrease in the magnitude of one or more of the constituents of a field. Decrease is obviously self-limiting. Either the diminishing variable will disappear, as the thyme has disappeared from the scrub-covered hill and the Algonquin Indian from Manhattan island; or the diminution will itself be checked or reversed. Increase, however, is also found to be self-limiting. The period of increase is succeeded by a period of 'steady state'; or by a reversed trend, usually resulting in an oscillation; or by a 'crash', in which the increase, often accelerating, is terminated by some sudden and radical alteration of the system. The first occurs when, for example, a local bird population is stablized by a limitation of suitable nesting-sites, or the number of lawyers in a small town by the number of their prospective clients. The second is exemplified by those linked oscillations in the numbers of prey and predators which have often caught the notice of ecologists; the lynx and the snowshoe hare in the Arctic tundra are a familiar example. Some forms of predation among humans show similar fluctuations. The third occurs when a tree growing on some steep slope outgrows the point at which its roots can support its weight and crashes down the hill – as once the last barrier crumbled to let the Thames flow through this gap and abandon its former bed. The

35

self-exciting expansion of an arms race between nations, or of sedition and repression within one body politic, usually results in similarly explosive change.

Finally, the ecologist develops the concept of *regulation*. When he observes 'steady state', he concludes that the forces interacting in his field of study are so disposed that any departure from the steady state tends to change the balance of forces in such a way as to reverse the departure. When he observes 'oscillation', he knows that the span of oscillation defines either the degree of displacement needed to trigger the change which will reverse the process, or the temporal lag before the reversal can become effective. When he observes increase or decrease, he expects it to generate regulative forces which will prevent its continuance in one or other of the familiar ways. Engineers will model for him all the patterns which he can observe in nature and at least some of the devices involved in regulation; in particular, those whereby deviations are 'fed back' into the system to check – or sometimes to multiply – the incipient disturbance.

All these concepts are familiar to the social scientist. The anthropologist describes the self-regulating devices which, in 'primitive' societies, regulate the size of the population, the exchange of goods, the division of labour, and the distribution of power; and he traces the disruptive effects, throughout such a society, of such changes as the introduction of firearms or gin or monogamy or a money economy, as the agricultural ecologist traces the repercussions through the whole rural milieu of chemical fertilizers or insecticides. The sociologist develops general concepts for understanding the dynamics of a social field. The stability of the sub-culture of West End, as Dr Ryan has described it, is ensured by the fact that every would-be leader within, every would-be helper from without, even every would-be deviant, is discouraged or neutralized or in the end extruded by built-in responses of the cutural ethic to the threats which the mere existence of such persons implies.

Ecology, as a science of interrelationships, has no use for the concepts of betterment, of value, or of choice. Men may release into the milieu a virus which destroys rabbits, and may develop a fertilizer industry which displaces sheep. No longer destroyed by sheep and rabbits, the coarse growth may displace the finer herbage. Woods may rise to overshadow their own seedbed so densely that only fungus will grow there. The self-destroyed wood may fall to let in the light and destroy the fungus. It is not for the ecologist to prefer beech trees to fungus or thyme to thistle. Equally value-free (at least in theory) to his impartial eye is the process whereby men build cities and cities attract men; cities breed plagues and plagues limit the size of cities; men curb plagues and cities expand into vast and formless aggregates, from which men try to escape. The automobile brings a means of escape for the few; the many follow and choke the roads. The roads multiply and let the traffic through; and roads and traffic carry with them the megalopolis from which they are flying. Ecology gives us a way of describing, not of valuing, the human process and its conscious and unconscious constituents.

Yet the human ecologist must take account, among the facts of his field, that men themselves are *valuers*. They seek and shun; and their seekings and shunnings are to be understood not in terms of the outer world, which the ecologist can observe, but in terms of the inner world which his subjects inhabit and which he may or may not share. In any field in which men function, the relevant facts and forces include not only what is happening but also what men think is going to happen; not only what they are doing to each other but also what they expect, hope, fear, from each other and from themselves. The inner world is fundamentally structured by human values.

It is thus a dynamic structure, a configuration of forces; and it behaves like other dynamic systems. Political beliefs, economic creeds, social attitudes, personal standards, change and develop partly in response to changes in the 'real' world and partly through their own dynamic interaction. As Professor Kenneth Boulding (1961) has observed, 'Such institutions as progressive taxation, inheritance taxes ... countercyclical fiscal and monetary policy, and the like, are in part outcomes of the socialist criticism of a pure market economy and in part the result of feedback of experiences ...' Nor can the rate of such changes be understood without reference to the resistance of the established ethic to changes of a kind *or at a rate* which would undermine its own coherence. Equally, the dynamic of the inner world may accelerate change. The drive to solve the problems created in America by racial and national minorities, problems which constantly recur in these papers – indeed, even the problems themselves – cannot be described without reference to the development of political and ethical ideas, in particular to the felt need to give adequate and viable meaning to the faith in equality.

In this value-structured world live, inescapably, not only the objects of the ecologist's observations, but also the ecologist himself. The writers of these papers are not only scientists. They are also as Dr Seeley has eloquently said, human agents, concerned with the 'quality' of the civilization in which they live and able to make – unable *not* to make – judgements about it of better and worse.

The most objective observer looks out from an inner world and through an inner world which structures and gives meaning to what he sees. This is as true of an astronomer as of an anthropologist; but the significance of the fact varies with the subject-matter. It is worth briefly following this variation along its course, which is punctuated with significant changes.

III

From their earliest recorded days men have wondered about the heavenly bodies and have woven around them a great variety of meanings, religious, scientific, and cosmological. Today, a vast body of coherent theory links our solar system with the remotest nebulae and begets increasingly daring speculations, which in turn evoke new observations to confirm or disprove them. This speculative search is an activity of the human mind which seems to grow with exercise; and the body of theory to which it has given rise is a mental artifact, a notable constituent of our inner world. It does not, however, affect, directly or indirectly, the subject-matter itself. Whatever may be the realities outside the astronomer's head to which his observations and speculations relate, they are not substantially affected either by his theories or by any action based on his theories – at all events, not yet. The celestial milieu remains an independent variable. For several centuries man's understanding of the solar system was blocked by his assumption that its motions *must* be circular, because circular motion was the most 'perfect'. The planets maintained orbits no less eliptical on this account; and when men belatedly discovered the fact, they had no means of bringing these orbits into line with their own aesthetic canons. Our inner view of the celestial milieu is a human artifact; but the universe itself certainly is not.

The terrestrial milieu is a different story. In the course of centuries of physical interaction, all intensively colonized land has become in some degree a human artifact. This valley where I sit was a swamp, until the river was controlled with locks and barrages. The depth and constitution of the soil are the product of a specific sequence of agricultural practices. Even the un-cultivated spaces usually owe their shape and preservation to the feudal system of land tenure which declared them 'commons'. This interaction has contributed to and been affected by an inner view far richer and more complex in content than that which we have of the celestial milieu. The changing face of rural England reflects changes not only in agricultural science but also in men's ideas of land as a source of power, of prestige, of security, of aesthetic satisfaction, and much else besides; and has itself con-tributed to these changes.

The physical city, 'urbs' – which Dr Deevey conveniently distinguishes from 'civitas', the city of rights and duties – is much more obviously and literally a human artifact. There is scarcely a physical object in it, from the skyscraper to the doormat, that was not born in a human mind and brought to being by human hands. It is also an artifact never finished, always in constant change; and it, too, is represented in our minds by a mental artifact, the body of our knowledge about and attitudes towards it. Between the physical and the mental artifact there exists the same elusive, mutual relation. Our ideas of it constantly change, both through our observations of it and through the development of our conceptions of what it might be and should be, and these changes in turn influence – perhaps very weakly, often mistakenly, and always with a critical time-lag – what it will become.

What then of 'civitas', the city of rights and duties – not merely legal rights and duties, but all the mutual expectations which make citizens of those who dwell in 'urbs'? The mutual expectations which create the sub-cultures of West End and Harlem and Puerto Rico are there to be studied, as Ryan, Fried, Ellen Lurie, and Hollingshead and Rogler have studied them. They are 'facts'; but they are primarily facts of the inner world in which these citizens live, a world which the observer may or may not share. The West End is a slum to the planners, to the residents a home. Which is it *really*? It is both, and much more besides. For these words describe not facts of the physical world but judgements proceeding from the value-structured inner worlds of the observer and the participant.

Thus, as our attention ranges from stars, through the physical world, to men and their doings, the inner world becomes increasingly involved, not merely as the screen, through which we look, but as an integral part of the material at which we are looking.

Of what does our inner world consist? Professor Boulding (1956) has described our inner view as 'the Image' and he has most usefully stressed its importance and its dimensions; but to picture the inner world we must look behind the image and ask what causes an individual or a society to see and value and respond to its situation in ways which are characteristic and enduring, yet capable of growth and change. A national ideology, a professional ethic, an individual personality, resides not in a particular set of images but in a set of *readinesses* to see and value and respond to its situation in particular ways. I will call this an appreciative system.

We know something of the ways in which these readinesses are built up. Even our eyes tell us nothing until we have learned to recognize and classify objects in particular ways; and there is little doubt that our conceptual classifications are built up in the same way. So, equally, are our values and our patterns of action. Our appreciative system grows and changes with every exercise of image-formation, a process normally gradual and unconscious; and like all systems, it is resistant to changes of a kind or at a rate which might endanger its own coherence.

These papers are a series of exercises in image-formation. Each includes its own individual *realization* of some aspect of the metropolitan environment as an ongoing situation and its own *valuation* of what is thus realized. Their major value, as I believe, is to speed in us who read them the development of our own appreciative systems, sharpening and revising our readinesses not only to see but also to value and to respond to the situation in which each of us is involved, in thought and will as well as deed, as agent as well as observer. Such a revision is overdue; for the last two hundred years have left us with an appreciative system peculiarly ill suited to our needs.

IV

During the past two centuries, men gained knowledge and power, which vastly increased their ability to predict and control; and they used these powers to make a world increasingly unpredictable and uncontrollable. This paradoxical result flowed from the fact that the technologies to which science gave birth enabled man not only to predict but also to alter the course of events in this milieu. Consequently, the outer world began to change in content, form, and complexity at ever-increasing speed, far outstripping the growth rate of any corresponding power of control. Hitherto, learning had meant adapting to the given. Now the very idea of 'the given' became suspect and dim.

None the less, the belief persisted that increased power to alter the environment brought increased control over it. This belief, still far from dead, is a manifest delusion. First, as every engineer knows, the difficulty of devising any physical control system lies not only – usually not chiefly – in generating enough power but also in generating enough information. Since the material world is a system, any change in the given is bound to have numberless, often unpredictable, repercussions thoughout the system; so even if the effect of the intervention is to bring under control the variable which is directly affected, the total system is likely to be less predictable than before, while all learned skills based on the former 'given' are depreciated. Further, these interventions, and the further interventions to which their unpredicted results are bound to lead, are likely to be self-multiplying. The rate of change increases at an accelerating speed, without a corresponding acceleration in the rate at which further responses can be made; and this brings ever nearer the threshold beyond which control is lost.

Even the most liberal legitimate statement of the faith is that men can learn to do anything that can be done by applying energy to material things. But this itself is of depreciating value, far less useful in America today than in the days of the expanding frontier. For the course of human activity in the last two centuries has been not only to change the physical environment from a relatively stable datum to an increasingly unstable artifact but also, and even more importantly, to replace the physical by the social milieu as the most important field of human interaction. It is highly doubtful how far the social environment can be either changed or stabilized by applying energy to material things – even, as these papers show, when the energy is applied to remaking urbs or suburbs.

In consequence, the last two centuries have ushered in a period of instability such as the world has never seen; a period, moreover, in which every new instability was either welcomed as 'growth' or accepted as the price of growth. The ecological view was obscured, overlaid, lost, even denied, by the new ideology of 'progress', with its implicit faith in the possibility of linear change which would not prove self-limiting. Furthermore, the idea of progress was itself confused by combining too uncritically the ideas of economic expansion and political betterment.

In the preceding paper I have tried to disentangle the concepts of expansion, betterment, and balance and to contrast the rival views expressed by Priestley and by Huxley. The difference is radical. According to the first view, an acceptable, even a 'paradisiacal' future will arise 'from the natural course of human affairs', even though (according to Marx) it lie on the other side of a bloody revolution which we cannot bypass and do well to speed. According to the second view, such a future will arise only as it is conceived by the insight and imposed by the will of men on the recalcitrant material of 'the cosmic process'. Marx is nearer to the Prince Consort than is Huxley to Priestley or the 1890s to the 1790s.

Yet all these views lack an ecological orientation. Priestley never questions that the natural course of human affairs is linear. Marx seems to have assumed that the dialectical process would 'wither away' with the State. Huxley does not envisage that the ethical process will have constantly to wrestle not only with the cosmic process but also with the unexpected results of its own activities. None of them seems to envisage enduring debate about the meaning of betterment, the direction of improvement.

We stand today amid the wreckage of these nineteenth-century hopes and certainties. Though the debate between the two views just illustrated remains unresolved, the second view accords more nearly than the first with the insight and spirit of our age. 'A worthy civilisation capable of maintaining and . . . improving itself' will not 'arise from the natural course of human

43

affairs'. It will need a 'constant struggle to maintain and improve' it. It will be a state not of nature but of art, man's great, composite work of art; and it can be no more noble than his dreams. We know, however, better than Huxley's generation what is involved in that endless struggle and what are its limitations.

V

The energy at our disposal has been multiplied and is now theoretically limitless. Our technology is sufficient to design and make far more than all the artifacts we are conscious of needing. Our means of communication are sufficient to transmit, store, and handle far more information than we can use. Increasing populations, increasingly urbanized, inhabit cities of increasing size, yet demand more space and more stuff per head with every year that passes. Man-made resources grow; natural resources shrink, especially the three most irreplaceable – clean air, clean water, and empty space. The ancient problem of equating populations with living-space and food supply emerges on a planetary scale. The problems of our day are set in ecological terms more strident, more blatant, more urgent, than ever before. They are how to regulate the instabilities inherent in this dizzy expansion; how to keep rates of change within bearable compass; how to choose between so many mutually exclusive possibilities.

Yet neither our institutions nor our ideologies are apt for such problems. Both still bear the shape impressed on them by the epoch that has closed; both resist, as every dynamic system must, changes which threaten their own coherence.

One of the most pervasive products of the ecological view is that every choice has a cost: for every realization precludes a hundred others. We can spend time, attention, life, like money, in only one way at a time; and, unlike money, these precious commodities are not expansible.

The cost inherent in every choice is most obvious in the use of land, for even the most modern technology offers no hope of expanding the surface of the planet. Demand multiplies and scope narrows. North Americans, whose grandfathers were still pushing out the frontier between primal nature and agricultural man, meet a new frontier coming back, an ever-narrowing net woven by their own realized dreams. The cost of every new development rises, not only in money, but in the abandonment, often for ever, of all alternatives. Land use illustrates with especial clarity the universal truth that betterment is not the accumulation of recognized 'goods' in an ever-increasing heap. It is the realization, within a dynamic system, of some *chosen* set of conditions to the exclusion of countless others.

How are such choices made? And what is the part of the planner in making them? Professor Webber gives a familiar Western answer. The planner helps by making 'explicit tracings of the repercussions and of the value implications associated with alternative courses of action'. The choice between them is not for the planner but for the agent whom he serves.

When the agent is the government of a large society, a State, or a city, comprising a diversity of 'interests', the choice is complex. The individuals concerned do not even know consciously all they want; even their individual wants may be mutually inconsistent; they cannot see ahead even as far as the planner, still less can they see as far as the executive's decision will commit them. How are they to arrive at a collective choice?

Professor Webber states a widespread view when he attributes any difficulties of collective valuation to the lack of a market. Where services are supplied through a market, the individual can express his own choice freely by buying or abstaining from buying; but where services are provided without direct charges, like education and roads and defence, the public must have some alternative means to express its opinion. How else can governments know 'what it is that customers prefer and hence what combination of services and facilities would benefit them and the community most'? In practice, governments must rely partly on the poor alternative of the pressure group, partly on their own

45

'value hypotheses' and those of their assistants who are 'able to make reasonably good judgements about the current preferences of some of the various publics'.

As an account of what actually happens, in America or else-where, in the making of collective choices, even through the market but far more in the political field, this account seems to me to miss an essential element. The men and women in England who abolished slavery, created the educational system, or gave women the vote were not acting on hypotheses of what the voters wanted. They were afire with faith in what people ought to want and in the end they persuaded their lethargic compatriots to give them enough support to warrant a change. American presidents, from Lincoln to Kennedy, do not speak with accents of inquirers seek-ing guidance about other people's preferences. Like most of the authors of these papers, they *criticize* contemporary values, urge *re*valuation, and appeal not to what people are thinking now but to what they ought to be thinking and would be thinking if they exposed themselves with sufficient sensitivity to the subject-matter of the debate. A free society is one in which these initia-tives spring up freely and in which men are free to espouse or resist them. It depends, like every other society, on the quality and abundance of these initiatives, as well as on the facilities for their debate, facilities which themselves depend partly on in-stitutions and partly on the capacity of the current appreciative system to criticize itself.

Again, as a description of what actually happens, the foregoing account seems to me to underrate what the planner does and must do. A plan, whether it be an architect's plan for the physical re-building of a city centre or an administrator's plan for a new mental health service, proposes a unique series of concrete, inter-related choices. It is a work of art, having already form but awaiting an executive decision to give it substance. It can be criticized, commended, compared with others; but the choice of the executive as such is limited to the plans before it. It may reject them all and tell the planners to think again; but in the end the planners will decide what alternatives shall be considered – and, by implication, will decide that all others shall be ignored. Only in the capacity of a planner can anyone propose a *new* answer.

'Government of the people, by the people, for the people.' How simple it sounds, until we explore the volume of meaning, different in each case, comprised in those words 'the people'. The responsibilities of 'government' are of many kinds and they fall differently on each one of us. We have all some responsibility for action, some area, however small, in which each of us and he alone can play the part of agent. There is a second field, wider and not congruent with the first, in which each of us can contribute to the making of policy. There is a third, wider still, in which each of us has power to give or withhold assent to the policy decisions of others. There is a fourth, yet wider, in which the only responsibility of each of us is the neglected but important responsibility of giving or withholding the trust which supports or inhibits our fellows in the exercise of their inalienable responsibilities, as their trust or distrust supports or inhibits us.

There is, however, a fifth field, sometimes merged in the first or second but in public affairs increasingly separated from them: the responsibility for planning, the creative function which shapes the work thus and not otherwise, whether the work be a building or an institution, a nation's history or a human life. Here lies the possibility for the vision that is manifest, for good or ill, whenever a 'state of art' is imposed on a 'state of nature', but which is only vaguely missed when it is absent: the authentic signature of the human mind.

Planning thus conceived is viewed askance by Western culture, in measure increasing with its scale in space and time. Large-scale attempts consciously to impose a state of art on human affairs have often ended disastrously; men's most enduring and approved achievements, both in the outer and in the inner worlds, have usually been the fruit of long, unconscious growth, deriving from the unhampered creativity of individuals. To guarantee scope for individual creativity unhampered by limitations physical,

47

historical, or institutional has always been an integral part of the American dream.

An ecological view helps us to understand what this ambition means in the conditions of today and what it will mean in the necessarily changed conditions of tomorrow; and how far these conditions might be controlled and at what cost. It does not encourage either arrogant hopes for social planning or easy optimism about the continuance of individual scope. The environment of the metropolis increasingly conditions us. Since it is man-made, we must acknowledge that through it we condition each other; yet, though it is a collective achievement, it does not represent a collective choice. Both its possibilities and its limitations are largely accidental; and it is a process in rapid change. How far could this process be directed? How far should it be directed – and in what direction? These papers supply no complete or coherent answers to these questions; but they contribute to our image of the process, and thus quicken and enlighten us for the debate from which answers may proceed. In particular, they help to pose those questions of value which are most easily masked.

For value questions tend to be masked beneath the vast ramifications of our instrumental judgements, judgements of how best to achieve some already agreed end. We are so good at know-how, and so deeply immersed in it, that we scarcely admit, except in the relaxations of leisure, the value of the act done or the work produced for its own sake. Yet, obviously, no instrumental judgement can be final. If A is worth doing only because it leads to B, then why B? And C? Ultimately, this regress must be closed by the judgement that something is worth doing for its own sake. Dean Rostow is right; whether the City Beautiful is or is not likely to breed gracious citizens, it is something which even moderately gracious citizens will want to build, because they will 'enjoy' it – and this none the less if they differ passionately in their judgements of beauty.

Again, choices based on major judgements of value tend to be masked behind the frequent threats latent in the instability of our

48

system. Too often, we can justify what we do by some manifest disaster that will otherwise overtake us. Watching a tyro on skates, staggering around in grotesque gyrations, each of which imposes the next, a spectator who asked, 'Why is he doing that?' might properly be answered, 'He is trying to keep his balance.' And indeed the pursuit of balance is enough to absorb the whole of the poor man's energy and attention. If, however, the spectator were to ask the same question about a master skater, weaving arabesques of bird-like elegance on the ice, it would be nonsense to make the same answer. True, the master, like the novice, must constantly seek a balance which must for ever be sought anew; for him, as for the novice, this is an iron law within which alone he can function. But the master has learned it so well that his obedience to it, unconscious for him and invisible to the spectators, is merged in the execution of what he is doing. He is *free* within the world of motion open to men on skates; and as a free man, his choice needs a different explanation.

Similarly a business, a city, a State, which bumps along from one crisis to another can explain and justify each response as the need to evade an imminent and lethal threat; but this is not the state in which human life, individual or collective, bears its most characteristic or its most gracious fruits. The stability of the *milieu intérieur* is only the *condition* of free and independent life. Its absence may explain a breakdown; its presence does not explain the achievement which it makes possible.

It seems to me that we sometimes elude the explicit value judgement also for a more fundamental reason. A hundred years have passed since Marx savagely denounced bourgeois morality as the rationalized economic self-interest of the strong. Even his critics recognized that there was uncomfortable truth in this. That it was not the whole truth seemed probable, if only from the fact that his theories failed to account for his own moral fervour or for the success of his ideas within the world of ideas. What alternative could his critics offer? Physical scientists who, encapsulated in 'objectivity', made increasingly daring excursions into 'nature', reported on their return that they found no 'values' in the 'real world out there'. Anthropologists and psychologists, exploring the behaviour of men and societies by methods as nearly scientific as might be, saw values as imposed by inner needs and outer circumstances through a determinism less crudely economic but not less rigid than Marx's age imposed on him. Neither physical nor social scientists could find a place for the creative originality of men *as agents* which their own activities so abundantly illustrated.

This was due, I suggest, to their unwillingness to accord even partial autonomy to that inner world which is structured and energized by human values. Happily, this difficulty which beset them as scientists seldom hampered their performance as human agents, for whom the making of responsible value judgements was an accepted major activity of life.

Human mental activity is indeed only part – a small and peripheral part – of the subject-matter of science. It is, however, equally true that the whole of science is only a part – a smaller and more peripheral part than we always remember – of human mental activity. Confronted with these two Chinese boxes, each of which claims to contain the other, we may conclude that the human agent is more than he knows and probably more than he can ever know.

To me, at all events, the view implicit in these papers is consistent with, and seems even to require an unshaken faith in, the power and duty of the human mind to make judgements of value – judgements which can never be validated, though they may sometimes be falsified, by appeal to any criterion other than another value judgement; faith qualified, none the less, by the knowledge that such judgements can never be final, that all dreams – even the American dream – must constantly be dreamed anew.

This paper first appeared as the concluding chapter to The Urban Condition, *edited by Leonard J. Duhl (1963). References in the text not otherwise explained are to other contributions in that book.*

REFERENCES

BOULDING, K. 1956. *The Image: Knowledge in Life and Society*. Ann Arbor, Mich.: University of Michigan Press.

BOULDING, K. 1961. *Conflict and Defence: A General Theory*. New York: Harper.

DUHL, L. J. (ed.). 1963. *The Urban Condition*. New York: Basic Books.

· 3 ·

The End of Free Fall

There is a story of a man who fell from the top of the Empire State Building; and he was heard to say to himself, as he whistled past the second floor, 'Well, I'm all right so far.' This story caricatures two absurdities into which we often fall. One is the absurd speed with which we come to accept as normal almost any outrageous condition, once we have actually lived with it, however briefly. The other is the absurd slowness with which we come to accept as real any impending change which has not yet happened, however near and certain it may be. Both tendencies are natural; they were indeed evolved for our protection. They only become absurd when they come to threaten us and all we value – as I think they are doing today.

Within six generations or so we in Britain – and others elsewhere even more quickly – have blown ourselves out of the agricultural into the industrial epoch, out of a rural into an urban way of life, and out of a natural into a man-made environment. The drive was supplied by exploding technology and by the novel institutions with which we exploded it and used its energy; but neither the technology nor the institutions which achieved the explosion are capable of dealing with its results. The main problems of a technological age are not technological but political and cultural.

The explosion released several critical rates of change. Populations began to multiply faster; individuals began to produce and consume more, to travel and communicate more, to expect and demand more. As a result they began to depend more on each other and, soon, to get more and more in each other's way; but these consequences were noticed only later, because the explosion began in a world so under-occupied and under-developed that for a time each change could excite itself and the others without breeding limitations. This is what I call the time of free fall. It grows clearer every day that the time of free fall is coming to an end. For the man-made environment in which the industrial epoch is enclosing us – created as it now is largely by the un-intended results of what everyone does – is becoming too un-predictable to live in and may soon become too unacceptable to live with. So if it is to survive, it will have to be controlled – that is, governed – on a scale and to a depth which we have as yet neither the political institutions to achieve nor the cultural attitudes to accept.

So the end of free fall (if we escape nuclear disaster) will probably not be like hitting the pavement but more like falling into a pond. We shall have to live in a much denser political medium. We must take account of the increasing mutual demands and expectations of people and societies who are growing more numerous, more crowded, more mutually dependent – but also, at present, more diverse and more mutually intolerant. This has already been happening, nationally and internationally, for long enough to invite a look ahead.

II

Let us consider first some of the more obvious trends which cannot go on as they are without defeating themselves and us; and then we can speculate about the changes which are likely to result from them or from the need to control them. The most obvious is the trend of population growth. The figures are becoming familiar, but they are worth repeating. It took about 1,650 years from the beginning of the Christian era for the world's population to double from about 250,000,000 to 500,000,000. With the beginning of the industrial revolution, the next double, to 1,000,000,000, took only 200 years. The next double, to

2,000,000,000, took only seventy-five years, which brings us to 1925. The next, to 4,000,000,000 is due, at present rates, ten years hence. The increase is greatest in those areas which are already most densely populated and least well fed.

Technologists may regard this as a challenge to the technology of food production. If we had free and unlimited power, so they claim, this planet could support – on the products of yeast factories and algae farms – as many as 50,000,000,000 people, a figure which at present rates will not be reached until the early 2100s or five generations hence. But this kind of speculation seems to me uninteresting, because the critical problems set by the trend are not technological: they are political and cultural. Long before food technology was defeated, the trend would obviously have set off a new battle for living-space on a scale not known before. Indeed, this battle is already on.

I do not necessarily mean the kind of struggle which submerged the Roman Empire under successive waves of wandering peoples, though there are still some artificially empty preserves where this might happen. What I have in mind is more universal: The right to deny immigration and to discriminate between immigrants is already becoming notably more important to the countries which attract immigrants, and more resented by the others. The attitude of the receiving countries is at present ambivalent, for their economies increasingly depend on colonies of alien labour which their cultures are unwilling or unable to absorb. This reluctance to admit will become even more marked if automation continues to eliminate more and more jobs in the lower grades of the employment pyramid. In any case, it seems inevitable – without some important political and cultural change – that the richer countries should continue for some decades at least to become even richer in relation to the poorer ones and at the same time to close their doors even more closely to immigration; and that in consequence both the pressure to enter and the resistance to entering should mount.

Suppose the barriers hold, and the struggle for the earth remains a national rather than an international one. In Britain the struggle for some place to live has already reached a new level of intensity. The present inequity between the minority who buy and own their homes and the majority who rent them or wait for them can only be remedied by measures more radical than those yet tried. The whole concept of land as an object of private property and profit must, I think, be on the way out in countries which are both developed and crowded. This concept was a product of the agricultural epoch, and it will be as inept in a world where land is over-scarce, as it was in the pre-agricultural epoch, when land was as over-abundant as the sea. Yet what an edifice of prestige and esteem, of security and independence, of speculation and profit-taking, still rests on land ownership; how successfully it has so far defended itself; what political, social, and psychological disturbances have always followed any effective attack on it!

But the struggle for the earth is not confined to the fight for a place to live. All kinds of necessary and expanding land uses – for industry, agriculture, transport, amenity – fight with increasing fierceness for diminishing opportunities. This fight is being transferred from the market-place to the political arena, because the conflict of values which is at issue involves the interests of many others beside the parties to a market transaction. But we have still to develop effective political ways of solving the more complex problem.

It is commonly claimed that medical technology will provide a solution for the problem of increasing population, long before food technology has been overwhelmed. It is true that medical technology, which has contributed so greatly to the population explosion, has made or will soon make conception much more widely controllable than it has ever been before, at least in those countries where the culture does not oppose the change. But whether the power of potential parents to regulate the size of their families will result in stable population – and, if so, how – is a matter which is uncertain, and wholly beyond the scope of technology.

The average size of family is an important factor in determining the size of population. It is also a sensitive one; in Britain today an average of three children per family would be far too high for stability and an average of two per family far too low. We do not know what determines the size of families, but if a sense of overcrowding became the effective trigger, it would be likely to work much too late and then too vigorously. The population would oscillate wildly between limits of perhaps increasing amplitude – a behaviour familiar to the engineers who design the control of automatic systems; they call it 'hunting'. But suppose, on the other hand, that at an overcrowded period the needs of unhoused families won overall priority; the best passport to a house would then be a large family and those penalized by over-crowding could escape only by making the overcrowding worse. (The feedback, as system engineers would say, would have become positive.) I offer no prophecy; I am only concerned to show that technological devices to control conception do not of themselves achieve or even make possible the stabilizing of a population.

Moreover, even a population which is stable in numbers would on present form continue to expand in other directions. Today's multiplying millions progressively take up more space and use more stuff per head. An American calculation (Paley, 1952), already more than ten years old, showed that in 1950 each in-dividual in the United States was using, directly and indirectly, eighteen tons of stuff each year, a rate not so far short of his own weight, every day, from birth to death; and this was expected to rise by 50 per cent in twenty-five years. Obviously, such a rate must soon run into practical limitations. On the way, it may or may not meet technological limitations; resources of raw materials might become exhausted; or energy supply might fall short of the increasing demand; or we might be defeated by the problem of disposing of waste. But even if we assume, as most technologists do, that every technological problem will always find its answer – and I see no conceivable reason why it should – there remain the political and cultural problems. These are inevitable, for this enhanced activity is taking place on the surface of a planet which is neither expanding nor expansible.

III

One aspect of these problems is urbanization. A hundred years ago only a negligible proportion of the human race lived in cities of more than 100,000. A hundred years hence only a negligible proportion are likely to live anywhere else. Even the United States, a country with an average population density less than one-twentieth of the United Kingdom's, has had to coin the word 'megalopolis' to describe conurbations, comprising many tens of millions of folk, united only by the fact that they live in a common warren; and of course other industrialized countries have them too. How are these aggregations to be planned? How governed?

The urbanization of Asia and Africa poses even more intractable problems which technology can set but cannot solve. For in the first half of this century, while the urban population of Europe and America increased two and a half times, that of Asia increased five times; and Africa's explosion may be even faster. The Ivory Coast is a country of only 3,000,000 or 4,000,000 people, speaking sixty-nine native tongues, none written and none mutually understandable; but the Ivory Coast capital, Abidjan, has grown in ten years from 10,000 to 300,000 – partly by a proliferation of multi-storey offices, air-conditioned hotels, and elegant residences, and partly by incorporating in its suburbs mud and straw villages which were traditional rural communities ten years ago.

We know well enough the social problems which were created in Britain by the urbanization of the nineteenth century, problems far harder to solve than the physical problems of public health. In Asia, still more in Africa, the disturbance created by this mass transition from rural to urban life is likely to be even greater. Meantime, in highly developed countries such as Britain, as the

Buchanan report has shown, continuing urbanization raises new technological problems which can be solved, in turn, only after further political and cultural change. The multiple purposes for which we have used our streets ever since medieval times will mutually frustrate each other within the next twenty or thirty years, unless we replan and rebuild our towns in wholly novel ways. But these new technological solutions are impossible without the new institutions needed to achieve them and the changes in cultural values which would be needed to support planning on such a scale. Even a temporary answer demands innovations more radical and more difficult than the technological innovation that posed the problem in the first place.

Other familiar trends present even sharper challenges. In Britain, already one of the most densely populated lands on earth, current forecasts show that the shortage of labour will increase over the next ten years. But in America, automation, on which our economic future also depends, is already said to be eliminating 2,000,000 jobs a year; and there already exists there a disfranchised class for whom the economy can at present provide support but not work. Nearly half their unemployed are young men who have never yet found a job. If this is to be the overall effect of increasing technological efficiency, what political and cultural change can we devise to give these millions an acceptable status – acceptable either to themselves or to their working fellows?

A related but distinct trend is the scarcity of particular types of skill. We are short of doctors, nurses, teachers, scientists, technologists, craftsmen. All these skills take several years to develop; so the number of those who possess any of them at any point of time depends on individual choices made several years earlier, by a process which is only slightly understood or controlled. And the distribution of these scarce skills between the places where they are needed – including their distribution between the public and the private sector – depends on a labour market which has become far too inflexible for this sort of regulation. This complex bit of political and cultural machinery, so necessary when it comes to maintaining technological momentum, seems clearly to be breaking down. What kind of change would make it work, or replace it with a better?

The general nature of all these political and cultural demands is clear enough. What is needed to keep the system going is a better mechanism for collective choices – both to make the choices and to put them into practice. These choices must commit ever larger numbers of people over wider areas of life and extend further into the future. Even so simple and marginal a matter as the future of motoring depends no longer on providing cars which people can afford to buy, but on providing roads; and hence on collective decisions not only on the pattern of the public road system, but also on how much resources, including land surface, to devote to roads – assessing this one demand against all the other demands that compete not just for public resources but for all resources. Individual choices through the market have generated a society which only political choice can regulate.

IV

The response to this demand has been visible in Britain for at least three generations. We can measure it roughly by the growth of the public sector. In 1850 the central government had eight departments of which four dealt wholly and one partly with external affairs. Five more departments were added in the next fifty years, eleven more in the first fifty years of this century, four more in the last three years. By 1956 more than one in five of the entire labour force were working for the central government, local government, or public bodies. Eight years later it is nearer one in three. It would be naïve to dismiss these figures as an example of Parkinson's Law. They record a massive and accelerating increase in the scope and volume of deliberate regulation of the national life. This has grown despite strong ideological resistance, and it now extends to the distribution of incomes, of services, of jobs, of homes; to education and health and welfare and transport – to economic planning and physical planning and social planning. It grows ever faster, yet few, I would think, would question that it fails ever further to keep up with its problems.

But it is in the international field that the lag in institutional development, by comparison with the growing need, has been most striking. In the past twenty years the number of sovereign States has more than doubled, almost entirely by the emergence of States without previous experience of self-government. In size, wealth, state of development, cultural type, and political ideology they are far more diverse than they were. Their potentiality for mutual destruction has increased immeasurably and their mutual hostility is certainly no less; yet their political and economic inter-action has increased many times. Against this huge increase in the need for international regulation we can set little by way of new international machinery. Means have been found, on American initiative, to give something away across national frontiers, a feat unknown on any serious scale before 1946. Yet if we reflect on the difficulties both of keeping the peace and of redistributing income within a single political unit – even one which has been developing a coherent political system for centuries – it seems clear that corres-ponding institutions in the international field do not yet exist and cannot yet be imagined though they are clearly needed now.

These are some of the more obvious trends to which we are so often urged to adapt; but some of those who urge us have naïve ideas of what adaptation means. We are men, not rats. It is through our societies that we survive and transmit the skills of survival; and it is equally through our societies that we create the oppor-tunities for human life and the skills to use and value them. Our major instrument of adaptation is government. T. H. Huxley, in a famous lecture in 1893, said: 'That which lies before the human race is a constant struggle to maintain and improve, in opposition to the state of Nature, the state of Art of an organised polity; in which and by which men may develop a worthy civilisation, capable of maintaining and constantly improving itself . . .' Nothing less than this, I suggest, is a worthy definition of human adaptation; and on that course there are cultural limitations and possibilities which I have not yet charted.

V

I have described our present state as the last stage in a free fall – the fall from the agricultural into the industrial epoch; from a natural into a man-made world; and so into an increasingly political world, a world so unpredictable that it demands to be regulated, nationally and internationally, by political decisions of increasing scope.

There is nothing defeatist in this conclusion. Government is our major instrument of adaptation. Just as we pride ourselves that through technology we have learned to shape the natural world to suit us, rather than suiting ourselves to it, so we shall pride ourselves, if we ever succeed in doing it, on shaping the man-made world to suit us, rather than scurrying about in search of ways to live with its vagaries. But we cannot pride ourselves on this yet, because we have not yet achieved it, nor have we evolved either the political institutions or the political ability to achieve it. Worse – we are not yet developing this ability fast enough even to keep pace with the course of events. This is not surprising, because political change is limited by the speed at which people can change their ideas of the world they live in, their expectations of it and their willingness to accept its expectations of them; and all of these I regard as *cultural changes*. Culture changes with the generations, but, as with other changes, there is a limit to the rate at which it can change without losing its coherence.

It is a fact strange beyond comprehension that the whole corpus of human knowledge is re-learned at least three times each century; and this becomes even stranger when we remember that what is re-learned is not only the technological skills and knowledge which serve our common needs, but also the political and cultural ways of thinking and feeling and acting which determine what we shall conceive our common needs to be, and how we should pursue them. Every one of us not long ago lay in a cradle, helpless and speechless, unable to distinguish one thing from another, even self from non-self, equipped only with a few reflexes, a unique genetic code, and a learning potential. Whatever we are now, our readiness to notice this and ignore that, to accept this as a commitment while we dismiss that as having no claim on us, to enjoy or accept relations of one sort and to hate and resent others – all this we have learned from our experience of the culture into which we were born; and it is increasingly this which determines how we shall accept and interpret new experience. This is the process by which each generation is incorporated into and inherits the society into which it is born, and through which alone it is socialized and humanized.

Yet how far from passive is this acceptance of the heritage! How selective are these learners, how much they amplify, change, or reject! For at least a dozen generations now, each generation has had more to transmit, to add, and to change than the generation before. This rate of change cannot increase indefinitely without breeding discontinuity with the past and ,incoherence in the present. That it has begun to do so is suggested by the increasing use of the world 'alienation' to describe the imperfect relation of Western man not only with his increasingly man-made world but with his neighbour and himself.

To capture some sense of this accelerating rate of change, we can let our minds run back over the generations. Politically and economically, we are already some way from Beveridge and Keynes; but how far were they from the generation before them which began the First World War with the slogan 'Business as usual', and which set up a committee on reconstruction to plan how best to return, after the war, to the social and economic conditions of 1914? Karl Marx is distant four generations, Bentham five, Adam Smith six. Eight take us to the Declaration of Right, twelve to the Elizabethans, twenty-seven to William the Norman, 100 to the builders of Stonehenge. About 300 generations have passed since the glaciers melted on what are now the

Cotswold hills. The linear ancestors of any one of us, back to the last ice age, would barely fill the first ten rows of the stalls in a modest theatre.

Let us consider only the first of those ten rows, the thirty generations that separate us from the England of Alfred the Great. Measure in imagination the difference in physical state, in institutions, and in culture between his England and ours, and divide by thirty. That is the measure of what, on the average, each of those generations accomplished, both in creation and in conservation. For each of these ancestors, born into his father's world and dying in the world of his children, was both a guardian of coherence and an artificer of change, sometimes sudden and violent change. From their hands to ours has come the triple heritage of environment, institutions, and culture which we are guarding, wasting, and re-making today, as they in their day guarded, wasted, and re-made it. For this heritage has no enduring substance unless it constantly be made anew.

This backward glance reveals much to encourage us. Britain twenty years after the Second World War seems in most human ways a better and more coherent society than it was twenty years after the First World War or twenty years after Waterloo – and Peterloo. For 150 years the political heritage and the cultural heritage have been growing to meet the demands of the emergent industrial epoch; and yet they seem to have more than kept pace.

Yet if my earlier analysis is right, we and our children and their children have a task which is harder now in several ways. The regulation of today's and tomorrow's world needs collective decision and collective action on a scale of space and time far larger than has ever been achieved or attempted before: it demands institutions, international as well as national, which do not exist, and cultural changes even faster than those which have already raised the spectre of alienation; and it will have to be done, in Britain at least, in conditions remote from those of free fall. To give more definite content to the cultural challenge, consider how the past generations understood and re-made in their day three

63

ideas which have been dominant in ours – liberty, equality, and fraternity.

VI

To at least the earlier half of those thirty ancestors, liberty meant the safeguard of specific rights to which persons of their class were entitled, and the corresponding restraint of other men's power, especially the public power. Of those nearer to us, some, widening the second half of the idea, aspired to make *all* power responsible; others, widening the first part, sought liberty in extending the area in which each could live as he pleased. None but the last generation would have conceived of including, among the liberties to which he aspired, freedom from the 'five giant evils' which our Welfare State was designed to combat – sickness, ignorance, unemployment, squalor, and want. Not even the last generation would have realized that, by this transition, the executive public power, which is still feared as the enemy and yet prized as the guardian of private liberties, had in fact also been acknowledged as their main architect.

And equality? For at least the first twenty of those thirty generations, equality was conceivable only in terms of the individual's place within a social order which was defined by nature and sanctioned by God. Only the last three or four would have conceived these social positions as theoretically open to all alike. Not even the last would have readily conceived the order itself as a human artifact, to be made and re-made, either blindly or knowingly, by the people whom it ordered.

And fraternity? All these generations knew the bond of fellow humanity that underlay differences of status and circumstance; but to earlier generations it had a stronger content within a narrower frontier. The Church might teach the brotherhood of man, but mutual dependence reinforced the lesson only within familiar groupings, bound by accepted ties and common culture and often consolidated by fear and hostility for the 'non-brothers' beyond the pale. Only the last few generations knew the 'mass-fraternity' of large national entities, or even of mammoth trade unions. Only the very last glimpsed the net of world-wide mutual dependence which underlies the mounting alienation of nation from nation. None had become conscious of the still nameless bond which links each generation to its unborn successors.

We and our children can keep what we value in our heritage only by re-making it even more radically and more quickly than our ancestors had to do. Ever more of our most urgent needs today can be met only through responsible choice made for us by others – not only by institutions and departments of State (as for example in implementing the Buchanan report sufficiently to give us towns in which it is possible to live) but equally by our ordinary fellow-citizens, who can block collective action by simply withholding their confidence and support. New forms of ir-responsible power dominate our world; for, as a recent writer (Rosinski, 1965) has observed, the creations of our own hands and minds have power over us by their very existence – the plant that *must* be used, the newspaper that *must* be filled, the in-stitution that *must* grow – and such power proliferates. Even our present degree of interdependence makes nonsense of the kind of freedom we are still conditioned to prize most highly.

The hierarchy of industrial roles distributes authority between our would-be equal selves at least as unequally, and sometimes less acceptably, than did the status structure of traditional society; and this hierarchy depends on a more unequal and specialized spread of skills and abilities. It may even have come to depend on natural abilities which are distributed so unequally that in the name of equality we are making societies in which many people can find no place. We do not know; for we are almost wholly ignorant of human variation, whether biological, psychological, or cultural, and our entrenched misconception of equality prevents us from using even such knowledge as we have. We are seeing only the first stirrings of that respect for human difference on which an adequate concept of equality may some day be based.

65

Fraternity claims for the first time a bond so wide in space as to lack reinforcement by what it excludes, and so deep in time as to include our responsibility to the future generations that we increasingly commit; and the claim appals us. It is no accident that our age has heard its most contemporary philosophy propound, through the mouth of its prophet, Jean-Paul Sartre, the sombre creed 'Hell is other people'. If that is true, the world into which we are moving will be hell indeed; and it will be true, unless we can give to fraternity an extension in space and time which has never seemed more remote.

In the man-made world beyond free fall, our children's first concern will probably be to establish sufficient authority to create their liberties. This will require them to exact from all an equality of responsibility more nearly corresponding to their equality of rights and to widen their sense of human obligation so that it extends not only across the frontiers of nations but also across the temporal boundaries of the generations, including the unborn. This will be a challenge to innovate and to conserve – a challenge more difficult, as I believe, than any which earlier generations have had to face.

VII

For the industrial epoch has opened as never before the two gulfs which in the past have always challenged most gravely the adaptability of mankind. One is the gulf between cultures; the other the gulf between generations. Even if within our own nation the ancient cultural gulfs are closing, the gulfs between the national cultures, in the world which technology is making interdependent, are at present so great as to exclude joint action which is even remotely equal to the needs of any of the participants; and the gulf between the generations compounds this cultural division and multiplies the threat to that cultural continuity which is the very medium of change.

In such a world, political and social life is likely to become more collective or more anarchic or, almost certainly, both. Communities, national, sub-national, and supra-national, will become more closely knit in so far as they can handle the political and cultural problems involved – and, in so far as they cannot, they will become more violent in their mutual rejections. The loyalties we accept will impose wider obligations and more comprehensive acceptance and will separate us by a wider gulf from those who reject them. These tendencies multiply around us now. A world in which interaction increases does not thereby necessarily become a more integrated world. On the contrary, these interactions may generate such tensions and pressures as to disrupt it. The worse the strains, the more demanding will be those societies which survive. Technology cannot unify the world. Unification, integration, are the fruits of political action; and the limits of political action are in the character and coherence of the cultures within which that action is taken, and in the rate at which those cultures can grow and change.

For us in Britain, some recent developments could prepare us to live in a multi-cultural world. One is the eclipse of our own once dominant position. Westminster democracy is clearly only one among several imperfect ways of governing a society. Christianity is one among several world religions, which together claim today the loyalty of a diminishing fraction of mankind. White is only one among several widely distributed colours of skin. These facts, which were always true, are no longer obscured, and they challenge us to find a more intelligent basis for loyalty to our own culture and for co-operation with others. This the social sciences can now supply, as they could not fifty years ago. We need no longer lack an understanding of the nature of our commitment to our own culture, and of others to theirs – and of the necessary limitations of them all.

Even the temporal boundaries of our awareness may be widening a little. It was only at the end of the eighteenth century, say five generations ago, that Western man seems to have awakened to the present significance of his own past. Only in the nineteenth did he become absorbed in the historical record, with ears attuned to hear in every age the persuasive voices of its own dead. Then, just a century ago, Darwin extended the historical perspective so far that recorded time became too brief to notice; and fifty years later Freud opened our eyes to an historical process in each individual life that links each latest development with its earliest past. As we are now so well equipped to sense the present significance of the past, it may be that we are not far from sensing the present significance of the future.

We are accustomed to distinguish so sharply between 'I' and 'not-I' and between 'now' and 'not-now' that any blurring of the dichotomy may seem unnatural to us; but this distinction also differs with the culture, and it is not immune to cultural change. When we learn to attach reality to others and to the future, are we not simply enlarging our idea of self to include new relations with others, and deepening the present in which we live to include more of the future which it always comprehends? These ideas may come more naturally to future generations which have learned to think of men and societies as systems of internal and external relations, extended in space and time and increasing in their selfhood through the extension of these relations.

And there is another way in which we are increasing our understanding of the continuity of life into the future as well as out of the past. Eric Erikson, in a recently published book (1964), discusses the human virtues. He defines them as those strengths which make humans human; and he describes how these virtues develop at different periods of life, each relying on the successful development of the one before. In infancy and childhood, according to Erikson, we have to develop hope, will, purpose, and competence; in adult life, love, care, and ultimately wisdom. In adolescence, linking the two, we have to develop one virtue only, which he calls fidelity, and which he describes as the ability to be true to self-chosen loyalties. I do not think I go beyond his ideas if I say that this stage covers the making of all those choices which lay the ground-plan of a system of values capable of growing for a lifetime without collapsing through incoherence, or becoming a prison through ineptitude.

This concept seems to me of great value, because it points beyond the relativity of particular values to the human quality or virtue which creates, preserves, and re-makes them; and also because it stresses the essential part which the sequence of generations plays in making possible this consistent transcendence of each generation's value system. The infant learns to hope in a milieu formed by the love and care and wisdom of a generation which was itself so nurtured; and only a generation which has learned in childhood hope, will, purpose, and competence to a degree seldom achieved today will be equal to building in adolescence a pattern of fidelities equal to its needs.

So the limits implicit in the rate of cultural change are not tiresome relics of the past for some social technology to eliminate. They are rooted in the most basic reality of our daily lives. They deserve the common allegiance of innovators and conservators alike. Our genetic heritage, as it seems to me, fits us not at all to live in the world which our technology is making; but we are evolving another, a cultural, heritage which, if we can understand it and be true to it, may yet enable us to realize the dream of T. H. Huxley, 'the state of Art of an organised polity...' When the first seed-bearing plants began to release their seeds to the wind's distribution, no mind could have foretold, if mind had been there to speculate, that, rooting and dying on the infertile wastes, their own decay would build up a bed of humus in which unimagined successors would evolve and flourish. We are guardians of a social humus more precious and more vulnerable than theirs – guardians not merely of values but of the soil in which values grow. That seedbed is today menaced by a vastly increased erosion. Conservators and innovators alike, our paramount duty to the future is to leave it a little deeper for our passage.

This paper was given as two broadcast talks on the BBC Third Programme and published in The Listener, *28 October and 4 November 1965.*

REFERENCES

ERIKSON, E. 1964. *Insight and Responsibility.* New York: Norton.

HUXLEY, T. H. 1893. Romanes Lecture. Published with Prolegomena in Romanes Lectures Decennial Volume 1892–1900. Oxford: Clarendon Press, 1900.

PALEY, 1952. *Resources for Freedom.* Report to the President of the USA by the Materials Policy Commission. Washington: US Government Printing Office.

ROSINSKI, H. 1965. In R. H. Stebbings (ed.), *Power and Human Destiny.* New York: Praeger.

Part Two

The Tower of Babel

· 4 ·

The Limits of Government

I am not a political scientist; only a student of communication, and, in particular, of the part which human communication plays in the regulation of human societies. This study leads back – or on – along two closely related paths. One is the study of systems generally, in the search for principles of regulation common to them all. The other is the study of communication generally, in the search for better ways of understanding those levels of communication which distinguish human societies from other types of system. These studies are new, many-sided, and rapidly growing; I claim no expertise in either. But they seem to be the fields in which I can most usefully think aloud in the presence of political scientists.

They have also a topical relevance, for they seem to me to provide apt language for describing simply and sharply the principal threat which shadows the world's political perspectives and the principal dimensions along which escape will have to be sought. I will first describe this threat as a breakdown in the conditions which make possible the regulation of political systems such as support us now. Then I will analyse this breakdown a little further, first as an ecological trap and then as a failure of communication.

II

Let me begin with a rather arid summary of what I understand by the regulation of a political system.

By a social system I understand a set of ongoing relations

between persons and organizations, governed by mutual expectations which are usually embodied in roles. It is, of course, a very
complex pattern. Each of us forms part of several sub-systems
and each of these is incorporated in varying degrees in others.
Whether we focus our attention on the family, the neighbourhood,
the city, or on the factory, the university, the trade union, we
distinguish something which we regard as a continuing entity but
only to the extent and in the field in which it maintains through
time two sets of relationships which are themselves intimately
linked – the internal ones which relate its members to each other
and the external ones which link it, as a whole, to its surround. The
entity is in fact a pattern of relationships, subject to change but
recognizably extended in time. This way of regarding the objects
of our attention helps to resolve the ancient dichotomy between
the individual and society and many other pseudo-problems
resulting from the tendency, built into our language, to regard
the objects of our attention as 'things', rather than systematically
related sequences of events.

Within this comprehensive picture I will distinguish a political
system as constituted by those relations which a society seeks to
regulate by the exercise of public power. This definition would be
too narrow for some purposes but it distinguishes one group of
relations which deserves a name. The departmental organization of
central and local government distinguishes a host of relations which
it is the function of these departments to regulate – the relation of
roads and road-users, houses and home-seekers, schools and
school-children, sickness and hospitals; the level of employment,
the balance of trade, the balance of payments, the balance of
international power, and so on. Every political activity is directed
to the regulation of some set of ongoing relations, whether internal
to the system controlled by the regulator or external, between
that system and other systems.

Regulation operates by manipulating one or other term of the
relationship or both. We may build roads or restrict traffic, build
schools or abstain from raising the school-leaving age, increase

the armed forces or cut our international commitments. Equally, of course, we may fail, partly or even wholly, in our regulative efforts. But even where we fail, I regard the relations in question as having been brought within the political system by the decision to treat them as regulable by acts of public power and thus to separate them from the host of other relations which are left to the regulation of the market or the family or of other determinants.

Even my casual list of examples shows how changeable is the content of a political system thus defined; for most of the relations it mentions were not regarded as necessary or even proper subjects of regulation a few decades ago. If we tried to distinguish the changes which forced these new regulative tasks on to the public power, we should have, I think, to distinguish at least three kinds, the physical, the institutional, and what I will call the appreciative. In the first I include all the physical changes of an island increasingly urbanized, mechanized, and populated; in the second, all the changes in the institutions by which we carry on our collective living. In the third I include all the changes in our ways of appreciating our situation; what we notice and what we ignore; what we regard as acceptable or unacceptable, important or unimportant, demanding or not demanding action by us. I regard this appreciative system as no mere derivative of the other two. They interact mutually and determine each other.

Consider one example. For many millennia the River Thames has earned its name as a continuing entity. It is in fact the way in which water from a stable catchment area finds its way to the sea. It expresses the relationships, changing but continuous, between rainfall, contours and porosity of the area, vegetation, and a host of other physical variables.

Throughout this time until very recently its valley provided a habitat for many species, including men, who long ago learned to live above its floodmarks and to cultivate its alluvial soil. Then we began to incorporate this river, once an independent variable, into our own man-made socio-technical system. We controlled its floods with barrages and dykes. We adapted it for transportation.

We distributed its water. We used it as a sewer. Our demands rose and began to conflict with each other, making necessary, for example, the control of pollution. Now these demands have begun to conflict in total with the volume of the river. We plan to supplement it by pumping out the deep reservoirs. Soon, unless some other solution appears, we shall be supplementing its flow by pumping desalted water from the sea. By then the Thames as an independent physical system, part of the given environment, will have virtually disappeared within a human socio-technical system, dependent on new physical constructions, new institutions, and a new attitude to the use of water and the regulation of the whole water cycle.

Regarding the content of a political system as the relations which it aspires to regulate, I will describe as its setting the standards by which these relations are deemed acceptable or unacceptable. Such standards are essential to regulation. The problems of the traffic regulator are set by the standard of congestion which is regarded as unacceptable. Without such a standard there would be no problem and nothing to regulate. All regulation depends on setting standards by a process of human valuation.

Many people dislike applying mechanical analogies to human affairs but I find it useful, for contrast as well as for similarity, to compare political governors with engineers before the instrument panel of some mechanical assembly. The engineer watches dials, each of which displays the course of some important variable, showing how closely it approximates to some desired standard or how dangerously it strays towards some critical threshold. These standards and thresholds are the settings of his system; and these signals of match and mismatch alert him to the need for regulative action. The picture serves equally for the political governor. He too watches the course of a limited number of variables – limited by his own interests in them and further limited by the number which he can usefully attempt to watch and regulate; and he too depends on signals of match and mismatch for his guidance.

There are differences also. The indices which the political

governor watches are for the most part not mere observations of the present state of critical variables but estimates of their future course, based on his latest knowledge of them (which is usually imperfect) and worked up by a process of mental simulation. A more important difference is that half his skill consists in setting the standards which he shall try to attain. For unlike the engineer, who controls a system designed to be controllable, the politician intervenes in a system not designed by him, with the limited object of making its course even slightly more acceptable or less repugnant to his human values than it would otherwise be.

In our society, as in many others, this setting has changed startlingly in recent years. The content of our political system – the sum of relations which we aspire to regulate – has grown and is growing in volume; and the standards to be attained have risen and are rising. The action needed to attain and hold these standards requires more massive operations, supported by greater consensus over far longer periods of time than in the past. On the other hand, the situations which demand regulation arise and change with ever shorter warning and become ever less predictable, as the rate of change accelerates and the interacting variables multiply. Clearly the task of the political regulator becomes ever more exacting.

By contrast, the capacity of political societies for accepting regulation is being eroded by several factors. The capacity for collective response is dulled, when the situation which should evoke it is not present to experience but is a mental construct, based on uncertain predictions. It is further dulled by those policies of collective security which cushion the individual against even such present experience as he might otherwise have. It is further limited by the need for greater consensus and by the increasing vulnerability of that consensus to the resistance of protesting or predatory minorities. Above all, it is limited by the emergence of time thresholds, which deny the opportunity needed for the gestation of innovation. These factors, some of which I will explore in greater length in a moment, create, as it seems to me, a wild and growing disparity between the least

77

regulation that the situation demands and the most that it permits. This is the dilemma which preoccupies me and which I want now to examine more fully from the two angles which I described earlier – first, as an ecological trap; and, secondly, as a failure of communication.

III

The first contribution we can draw from the study of other ecological systems is that these gloomy anticipations, even if they were fully borne out, would be in no way surprising. We have no reason to assume that political societies will prove to be regulable at any level which we would regard as acceptable. Many species have perished in ecological traps of their own devising. We may already have passed the point of no return on the road to some such abyss.

A population in a favourable but unfilled habitat normally multiplies at a constant rate until it meets or breeds limitations which slow and in time arrest its further growth. It may then stabilize, at or below its maximum, in the same or an altered form, with oscillations of less or greater amplitude; or it may even disappear, because in its period of expansion it has either unfitted itself for life in a limited environment or unfitted its environment to support even a limited population. These are the ecological traps I mentioned, in their most acute form. We call them traps only because our interest is engaged by the species they ensnare. From other viewpoints, such as an interest in the continuance of organic life, the replacement of one species by another is of no importance or appears as a salutary bit of regulation. If our kind exterminates itself and leaves an earth habitable only by creatures tolerant of a high degree of radiation – cockroaches are, I believe, favoured for the succession – only a judgement which values man and his works will notice any serious discontinuity. But we are human and we must take our human value judgements seriously. Here again we are reminded that all our thoughts about political regulation assume and depend absolutely on our human value judgements.

Not all species have worked themselves into ecological traps; many – the trilobite and the porcupine are stock examples – have established a stable relation with the milieu which has supported them for millions of years. In the past many human populations have similarly attained and held, for periods respectable by our human time-scale, a state of dynamic balance with their milieu, including the other species with which they shared it. Men have shared the Amazonian jungle with its other fauna for several millennia, without substantially changing the jungle or their neighbours or themselves.

The stability of these societies results from the fact that their way of life does not of itself disturb either the milieu or the society itself in its physical, its institutional, or its appreciative aspect. Each generation, taking over the skills, the institutions, and the ideas of the one before, finds them as apt as ever to the milieu in which they have been developed and the purposes which they have been designed to serve. They may in time become inept through some independent change in the environment, slow or sudden – an eruption or a change of climate, an incursion of predators or the impact of a foreign culture. But no significant change is generated by the activities of the system itself.

In the history of the human race, stability in this sense has diminished towards a vanishing point which, I think, is now in sight. The skills, the institutions, and the ideas of hunting tribes served their needs far longer than did those of agricultural peoples, because they did not generate the changes which would have made them obsolete. Even the agricultural epoch, those last three hundred generations which span the whole era of recorded time, gave birth to civilizations which deserve to be called stable over several centuries, in that their skills, their institutions, and their ideas did not change rapidly from one generation to another. We now seem to be approaching a point at which the changes generated within a single generation may render inept for the future the skills, the institutions, and the ideas which form that generation's main legacy to posterity – and the next generations' principal heritage. If this is true, it looks to me like an ecological trap identical in character with those which I described earlier, though the determinants of the trap are social and cultural, rather than biological.

IV

But is it true? The analogy is obviously far from exact. Ecological traps arise because biological evolution works too slowly to adapt some species or population to some environmental change or rate of change. Need we assume any significant limits to the far more rapid processes of cultural and political development?

I think we must. The reasons appear when we define the conditions that make regulation possible. They are, I suggest, four.

First, the regulator must be able to discriminate those variables that are involved in the relations it seeks to regulate and to predict – or control – their future course over a period at least as long as the time needed to make an effective response.

Secondly, it must be able to preserve sufficient constancy among its standards and priorities to make a coherent response possible.

Thirdly, it must have in its repertory or be able to discover some response which has a better than random chance of being successful.

Fourthly, it must be able to give effect to this response within the time which the first and second condition allow.

Some would add a fifth condition – that the results of the response must be sufficiently distinguishable in the future course of affairs to prove or disprove its aptness and thus give the opportunity to learn by trial and error. I do not include this, because it seems to me that in important political decisions we often must and do get on without it. The results of most of our important decisions return to us long after the event, in manifold and often unrecognizable forms and indistinguishably mixed with other changes; and even when we think we can trace them, we cannot compare them confidently with what would have been the results of any alternative decision we might have taken; for at these we can only guess. I suppose we do learn something from experience, even in politics; but the process is so obscure and so seemingly remote from the ways in which we learn from simpler and more repeatable experiences that I will omit from consideration the limitations which are involved in this condition, except in so far as they are also involved in the other four.

The other four conditions are limiting enough. The most obvious disparity is between the 'lead times' needed to mount any regulative action and the future span over which any reliable prediction can be made. The first grows ever longer; in important fields, such as changing land use and changing educational needs it is reckoned in decades. The second grows ever shorter; changes unforeseen a year before may make nonsense of well-matured plans which already commit huge resources. Plans for the re-organization of ports have recently been made obsolete by developments in 'containerized' transport. Examples could be multiplied. It is quite possible for the world as we know it now to become unregulable in important fields, in that it might pass the point beyond which *any* considered action might have a statistical probability of being worse than random. There are many situations in which to be systematically late is to be systematically wrong.

But the condition which produces this unhappy result is not primarily due to exploding technology but to the limitations of human communication. The long lead times which intervene between the emergent need for action and its achievement are partly due to the delays inherent in the processes of generating a sufficiently agreed view of the situation, a sufficient consensus on the course to pursue, and sufficient common action to achieve it; and all these are collective processes, mediated by communication. Even the confusion and loss which rapid technological innovation produces by its unplanned impact on other parts of the process only express a human failure to achieve, at that level, that phasing of complex activities which, at simpler levels, is recognized as a proper technological necessity and a proper technological skill. The far more difficult conflicts between nations, classes, and cultures – between rich and poor, communist and anti-communist, Negro and whitey, Arab and Jew – remain insoluble so long as they reflect the lack of any common basis for communication. Technology has made this lack into a threat, by reducing the distance between cultures and increasing the distance between generations; but it did not cause the lack and it cannot abate the threat.

Since until recently science has tended to blind us to the extent to which all our activities – including science – depend on communication, it is worth recalling that human societies differ from others primarily because humans talk and even listen. Nearly all we know comes from communication, rather than from observation or direct experience. Even the ways in which we classify experience were taught us through communication; most of them are inherent in whatever language we use. Our interests and our standards were formed largely through communication; the rebel, the deviant, and the prophet, no less than the most conforming member of the Establishment, define themselves, by protest if not by compliance, by reference to the specific culture which made them human, by claiming them from infancy as members of a specific communicative network. No one can make another do anything at all, except by the obscure process of communication. Even an atom bomb, we are told, is valued for the sake of the message it sends out while it is intact, rather than for the energy it would release if it went off. Change and stability in human societies are mediated hardly at all by those transfers and transformations of energy with which we model the physical world, almost entirely by those transfers and transformations of information which physicists have at last learned to distinguish and have thus made respectable subjects for scientific speculation.

V

Since we depend absolutely on communication, within societies, between societies, and between the generations, developments which threaten these communications with failure are a lethal form of trap. By failure of communication I do not mean failure in the means to transmit, store, and process information. Of that we have already more than we can use. I mean failure to maintain, within and between political societies, appropriate shared ways of distinguishing the situations in which we act, the relations we want to regulate, the standards we need to apply, and the repertory of actions which are available to us. This fabric, on which communication depends, is itself largely the product of communication. Demands on it are rising. We need to consider what chance there is of meeting them and at what cost; especially at a time when new techniques for handling information are finding their way into the regulative process at all levels, based on assumptions about how that process works which are not, I think, well validated and at the same time changing the process more deeply than we realize.

So let me turn to the threatened failure of communication in the three roles I have mentioned – its role in defining problems, in evaluating programmes, and in securing co-operation and concurrence.

First about the way in which problems are defined. In more static societies the relations to be regulated and the situations which involve them are usually familiar and are often equally visible to all. In our society, the more numerous relations to be regulated combine in subtle and often novel ways and the situations which involve them have to be anticipated by techniques of simulation, often involving the combination of large volumes of information. So the task of defining the problem is by no means simple. Ways of seeing the problem become obsolete, no less than ways of solving it.

To revert to an earlier example, it was possible until recently to think about the distribution of water in southern England, while taking for granted both its supply and its disposal. Today, distribution can be usefully considered only as part of a much wider problem – hence, among other things, the merging of river and water authorities and the setting-up of a water resources board.

It was possible until recently to think of traffic regulation simply in terms of better roads. Today, as Professor Buchanan has so lucidly shown, it makes no sense except as part of the problem of providing buildings with accessibility and thus as part of the still wider problem of three-dimensional town planning; for towns contain and relate the buildings where all journeys begin and end and of which accessibility is one among many necessary attributes, none of which can be fully enjoyed without denying others. Town planning, in turn, cannot be usefully approached until we have rid our minds of the concept of a street as a multi-purpose space, a concept as inept today as the multi-purpose great hall of a medieval house would be to modern domestic living.

This need constantly to restructure problems makes novel demands on communication. For policy-making is a collective activity and the first condition of the communication which makes it possible is that the participants should be talking about the same thing, or at least should know when this is not so. Most of the discussion which goes into policy-making is directed to reaching agreement on how the situation can most usefully be regarded; in other words what is the complex of relationships most significantly involved. Policy-making is vastly complicated when this cannot be taken for granted but must constantly be reviewed.

A very simple example is provided by the efforts made in Britain and in the USA to co-ordinate the policies of the three fighting services into a single defence policy. Fifty years have passed since the war which added a third fighting service and made it apparent that all important future activity in that field would be combined operations. Yet neither country has yet succeeded in fully establishing what I will call a common ideology for the three services. Where this is lacking, the participants in the potential dialogue lack in

84

effect a common language in which they can fruitfully disagree – a condition which is by no means confined to the fighting services.

The situation to which the policy-maker attends is not a datum but a construct, a mental artifact, a collective work of art. It has to be simplified, or it becomes unmanageable; yet if it is over-simplified, it will be no guide to action. It has to reflect present and future reality; yet if it departs too sharply from the familiar thinking of the past, it will not be sufficiently shared by those for whom it has to provide a common basis for discussion. It has to be not merely discovered but invented, not merely invented but chosen from among several alternative inventions, each a valid but differently selected view. Most difficult of all, it must not obscure the views which it supersedes.

Crime, for example, has long been regarded as a violation of the social order, demanding correction, and a violation of the moral order, demanding expiation. We have learned to regard it also as being, sometimes, a cry for help, demanding response, and a protest against the social order, demanding attention. Each of these views invites action partly inconsistent with the others; yet we cannot afford to suppress those on which we cannot act.

Thus the definition of political problems becomes more difficult as the relations to be regulated become more numerous and involve more diverse conventional views. The more thorough the analysis of the situation, the more complex it is found to be; and this complexity consists in the variety of inconsistent values which call for optimizing or at least satisficing. The problem of 'traffic in towns' as it was handed to Professor Buchanan looked far simpler than the problem which he handed back to the policy-makers. His analysis disclosed the multi-valued choice latent in any adequate analysis of 'the situation'.

VI

Now for the evaluation of programmes. Here again it is convenient to look first across the Atlantic. For as you know, the defence department of the US government has pioneered the application to government procedures of methods first developed in industry during and after the last war, to increase both 'efficiency' and 'effectiveness'. Added interest attaches to these methods because of the President's direction that other departments should adopt them. They are clearly and modestly described in a little book recently produced by the Rand Corporation (Novick, 1964).

The object of these procedures is, first, to ensure that action serves policy; secondly, to improve the information on which to choose between one programme and another; and thirdly, though much more modestly, to improve the information which may help to guide the distribution of resources between one field of policy and another. These objects are to be attained by budgeting activities according to the policies they are supposed to serve, rather than according to the departments which carry them out; to budget them over periods long enough to disclose their real costs and benefits; and to interpret costs and benefits according to the meaning which policy gives them. Benefit means success in implementing the policy concerned; cost means the loss of whatever else the resources so used might have achieved.

This may not sound revolutionary; but it is. Its first finding is to dispel the assumption that action now in train serves any policy at all. This is not to be assumed. It may have become self-perpetuating. It may serve some policy long abandoned or some purpose which some other policy is designed to frustrate. It may be an expression of empire-building or Parkinson's law, of pure competitiveness or the tyranny of technological or administrative fashion. These risks are not excluded by the present system of annual budgets for action departments. These may be needed for other purposes but they are inept for keeping action in the service of policy. They should be subordinated to a separate system of long-term programme budgeting.

The procedure depends on and assumes the clear, prior definition of policy in terms of objectives. This, the memorandum insists, is a primary, creative act of choice, with which the programme-budgeter cannot help. For choice involves valuing, and valuing is by implication excluded from the rational process. No calculus can compare the relative values of atom bombs and medicare; or even those less dramatic disparates which trouble the policy-maker at every level, such as the relative importance of improving primary or secondary education. The programme-budgeter can answer no question of value. All he can do is to 'sharpen his (the policy-maker's) intuition' by telling him what he may expect from what he is doing or contemplating now and what he might hope to achieve by applying the same or different amounts of resources in some other way.

So to benefit from this procedure, the policy-maker must set his own house in order. He must define his objectives and group them in a small number of fields, which should be so far as possible distinct. The memorandum recognizes that these are searching requirements, for it treats as open the question how far this procedure will prove applicable to civil policy and civil departments.

For, first, the grouping of objectives is itself a creative act, affecting both how they are seen and how they are valued. It determines which shall most actively compete and which of the policy implications of any proposed action shall be most effectively hidden. Within the defence department, it was relatively easy and obviously useful to group together, for example, all weapon systems which contribute to a policy of strategic retaliation, irrespective of the service which controlled them. Similar groupings in the civil field might prove more arbitrary.

Further, however objectives are grouped, they will overlap. Water conservation is an aspect of agriculture and of health, even of agricultural price policy, as well as the conservation of a natural resource. Yet the development and conservation of natural resources has a strong claim to be considered a major policy field in its own right.

Thirdly, however policy fields are grouped, they will not coincide with the boundaries of departments organized for action.

87

There is at present in the United States no Secretary of State responsible for the conservation and development of natural resources; and if there were, he could not gather into one executive department activities which today are divided between eleven.

You will notice that this procedure bears the marks of its origin. It does not distinguish between objectives to be attained once for all and standards to be maintained through time, which I regard as a more adequate description of the setting of a regulator. It assumes that the policy-maker's only problem is the apportionment of scarce resources between conflicting claims. It does not take account of possible conflicts between the objectives themselves – for example, between defence policy and other aspects of foreign policy. It therefore assumes that costs and benefits can be usefully, if not completely, calculated in terms of the policy which the action is designed to further and need not follow its endless repercussions in other fields – except, of course, the repercussions of its claim to resources. (This is reflected in its more commonly used name of cost-effectiveness.) It assumes, in brief, that planning and programming involve the comparison of different means to attain an agreed end, the means being neutral.

Now though this is not true even in industry, still less in defence, it is, I think, a more useful assumption in those fields than in the fields of civil policy; and it may well be that methods devised to evaluate weapon systems will prove inept to evaluate poverty programmes. But these simplified methods should not on that account be dismissed. Some simplification there must be – and therewith much exclusion and distortion. It seems to me none the less useful to experiment with them, both to explore the limits of their usefulness and to discover what passes for planning in their absence.

In the meantime we should not assume that programme-budgeting models the process by which all plans and programmes are compared. Even a chess-playing computer, I understand, when involved in the complexities of the middle game, cannot guide its play by a strict analysis of costs and benefits but has to rely on general principles. And unlike chess, politics, except perhaps in the defence department, is not a 'zero-sum' game: indeed, is not a game at all, in that it has no built-in measure of success.

Thus programme-budgeting, as I have so far described it, is a procedure designed not for regulators but for operators, seeking defined and single-valued objectives. This, however, is not all: for as the Rand memorandum candidly puts it, 'programme-budgeting begins with structuring the problem'. The programme-budgeter, in other words can help the policy-maker to define what the problem shall be deemed to be. If he wishes to define the problem in a way with which his budgeting techniques can deal, he will do his best to have it simplified to the pursuit of one de-fined, single-valued objective. If on the other hand he uses his analytic skill as for example the Buchanan committee used theirs, he is likely to define a problem of multi-valued choice which will defeat his budgetary techniques.

Thus the multiple analytic skills of the programme-budgeter reveal a dilemma inherent in the policy-making process. The more crudely simplified the objective, the more efficiently it is likely to be pursued. Given a single-valued objective and a repertory of 'means' assumed to be comparable simply by their cost in resources, it may be possible to demonstrate objectively which means is the 'best'. But no political problem can or should be stated in these terms; the more truly we present to ourselves its multi-valued nature and the multi-valued effects of all the means by which we might pursue it, the more impossible it becomes to compare either the costs or the benefits of alternative solutions.

The solution to any multi-valued choice is a work of art combining in a unique way the regulation of the various relations involved. The problem of the policy-maker is to choose between such solutions (if he is happy enough to have more than one to choose from) or boldly to tell the planners to think again. But he cannot tell in advance what combination will prove attainable or even preferable. The Buchanan report, for example, discloses to him the values which he needs to combine, the time-scale on which he should think, and the limitations which he should not forget; but only a definite plan for a defined area can show him one of the unnumbered combinations between which, if he knew them, he might choose. A foreign policy, an educational policy, no less than a development plan, if they are to be more than a reaction to the most obvious pressing danger, need to display the characteristic qualities of a work of art – and call, in consequence, for common attitudes, as well as skills, in those who assess and support them, no less than in those who design them.

VII

I come to my third query; the role of communication in securing the concurrence needed to carry a policy into effect. In concurrence I include everything from understanding commitment to grudging acquiescence, so long as it secures what is needed from the individual concerned. We do not know much about the many and various ways in which communication secures agreement or exacts obedience but we can recognize situations in which its task becomes harder and the illustration I have just used supplies one example.

Since programme-budgeting requires the policy-maker to group his objectives in fields which cannot correspond with the boundaries of departments organized for action, it follows that each executive agency must expect to implement more policies and to frame none; and that each policy-making authority must rely for the implementation of its policies on more executive agencies and must expect to control none. This is bound to make more acute, within the regulator itself, the ancient problem of controlling executive power.

We already know this problem. Policy-makers insist, if they can, on controlling the departments which implement their plans, because, as mere co-ordinators, their communications are usually too weak to support their responsibilities. Even the 'overlord' with overriding executive authority over several departments often has a hard struggle to assert it. We may well conclude, then, that if action is to be subordinated to policy, the power of communication to secure agreement or at least to exact obedience will have to be enlarged.

This raises a further problem, when we recall that the making of policy and its execution involve the same people in radically different kinds of communication. The making of policy, especially in times of rapid change, involves continuing dialogue, based on readiness to question familiar assumptions and to consider the radical restructuring of problems. The execution of policy requires the acceptance of decisions and the co-ordination of long-sustained action in their service. These sharply different roles cannot be divided between a hierarchy of policy-makers and what I have heard called a 'lowerarchy' of executants. Everyone concerned must to some extent share both, including those outstanding executants who tend to be found in the seats of power in all executive departments. The two roles can be combined, I suggest, only within a sub-culture which highly values both and protects both by a disciplined consensus, quick to react against the infringement of either. Such a consensus is sometimes found within a small highly trained, highly motivated service. Is it possible or even desirable in a large, complex political society?

For of course both the dialogue by which policy is made and the action by which it is implemented involve the governed also; and here too the demands on communication are rising. So naturally we are seeing an immense, half-conscious expansion both in the machinery for mediating dialogue and in the machinery for securing acquiescence. On the one hand, the traditional role of Parliament is being supplemented, if not superseded by formal and informal consultation between government and governed, notably organized business and organized labour. On the other hand, government is extending the traditional areas in which it can make its communications relatively effective.

To its own agencies it can issue executive instructions which are almost sure to be obeyed, since those who receive them are committed by their roles to obey them or resign; and if they fail to do so, they can usually – not always – be replaced. As we all know, this field of executive authority is growing apace. It is being further extended by government's increasing control over the private sector, through commercial contracts and those other manifold means of incentive and deterrence which Andrew Shonfield (1965) has traced in his book on Modern Capitalism. In addition to all these controls which need no legislative sanction, government can promote legislation, which it can be almost sure of passing, to alter the distribution of benefits and burdens, change the rules by which life is lived, and even extend its own executive powers; and here too its accumulated powers are growing. To these powers we must add the persuasive powers which radio and television have multiplied and which all governments increasingly use both to spread their own appreciation of the situation in which they are acting and to secure the co-operation they want.

This growth of power alarms many, as well it may; but we can evaluate it only in the context of the dilemma which I have described within the machinery of government and which is writ even larger in the relations of government and governed. The same nexus of communication must mediate both the dialogue which keeps policy under review and the co-operation which allows it to be executed. Within the government machine, oriented as it must be to action, the chief danger may be that the momentum of action will defeat policy-making. Between government and the governed, the more threatening danger may be the opposite; that the debate on policy will frustrate any sustained action. Either would be lethal, both can be excluded, I suggest, only by the kind of consensus I have described, sustained at national level. This in these days can be sorely tried. The agonies of American admirals and generals, which the procedure of congressional committees allows us to share, are similar in kind but, I think, far less radical in their scope than those which beset many responsible trade unionists in Britain today, invited to revise their attitudes to collective bargaining as only one of several competing 'values'.

The dialogue between government and governed has become an immensely difficult exercise in communication. First, it involves much more searching demands on the governed. I said earlier that in principle we can regulate our relations with the milieu by manipulating either the milieu or ourselves. The first is more comfortable and more congenial to a technological age but the second is increasingly the pattern of the future. To control the flow of the Thames we had only to discipline the river but to control its pollution we have to discipline ourselves and this transition is typical of what control will increasingly mean.

Further, this dialogue becomes more comprehensive; for all a government's actions are themselves communications, demanding explanation. When unemployment was not deemed to be regulable, people responded to losing their jobs by finding others, if possible in other and perhaps more stable occupations. When they lose their jobs through what they regard not as an act of God but as an act of State, they may respond differently. A doing is not the same as a happening. It is a message, as well as an event.

Thus every government becomes involved in an endless exercise of explanation, the difficulties of which are enhanced by the three factors I have examined. The situation is often a novel view of the relations to be regulated, not yet shared by all parties to the dialogue. The solution, if commended by an adequate 'cost-benefit' analysis, will almost certainly not be the one which those most concerned would favour – still less, if it relies on the more aesthetic criteria on which we fall back when cost-benefit analysis fails. And its implementation will sometimes require wider concurrence than the traditional powers of government can achieve, even extended as they now are.

So the crucial purpose of the debate is to generate trust or distrust. And this – perhaps the most important political function of communication – depends not only on the constraints which are placed upon criticism but also on the incentives which are offered to it by the shape of political institutions. The fact that in this country we have at all times an alternative government in being and more or less identified mobilizes the attack on the government's credibility in a way which is I think peculiar to us. Consider the relatively sheltered position of an American president compared with a British Prime Minister.

VIII

Clearly, the demands on communication are rising in the regulation of political societies, both within the governmental regulator and between it and the governed. Can we hope that increased understanding of this essentially human art and increased skill in its use will match the rising need?

The traditional means of making people do as they are told are weakened in practice and discredited in principle. On the other hand, more potent and subtle means of moulding opinion and attitudes are available. Whether these formidable engines will be either properly controlled or properly used remains at present, I think, an open question.

Our former means of estimating the results of actual or hypothetical courses of action have been enormously extended but at present they serve single-valued rather than multi-valued choices and are likely, I think, to reinforce the tendency to over-simplify which always besets harrassed regulators when faced by multivalued choices. They are designed for operators, rather than regulators. It is no accident that they entered the machinery of government through the defence department.

On the other hand, they have vastly fortified the process by which situations are defined, and the readiness to redefine them. And this is of the greatest value at a time when traditional definitions of situations and traditional attitudes towards them are becoming increasingly inept.

This in turn affects the structure of the appreciative system on which all communication depends. In the political context it is a solvent of ideologies. But communication is also a builder of ideologies. It is, I think, in its impact on political ideology that our increasing understanding of communication is most important.

We have come a long way since Condorcet, waiting for the guillotine, could look forward to a day when the sun would shine on a world of free men with no master but reason. He did not doubt that free men would find in their reason a sufficient guide to what T. H. Huxley was later to call 'the state of Art of an organised polity'. How much more modest is the role allowed to reason in the Rand memorandum, blandly relegating all questions of value to human intuition!

If indeed we have reached the end of ideology (in Daniel Bell's phrase) it is not because we can do without ideologies but because we should now know enough about them to show a proper respect for our neighbour's and a proper sense of responsibility for our own. The critique of ideology is I believe the most important political function of communication; a critique which needs to be creative and conservative no less than destructive. These self-spun webs alone support us in the abyss of non-humanity. Major operations on them are fearful enterprises. We shall be better equipped for such enterprises if we share a common understanding of the strange fabric we are working on and the still stranger instrument we are working with.

This paper was originally given as a lecture at the London School of Economics and Political Science on 22 November 1966, under the title 'The Regulation of Political Systems'.

REFERENCES

NOVICK, D. (ed.). 1964. Program Budgeting. Washington: US Government Printing Office.
SHONFIELD, A. 1965. *Modern Capitalism.* London: Oxford University Press.

· 5 ·

Planning and Policy-making

Two doubts seem to shadow the future working of our political institutions. One concerns the institutions needed to make any policy appropriate in scale to the needs of our situation; the other concerns the institutions needed to implement any such policy. Both stem from the increasing complexity of our situation, the increasing speed and unpredictability of its changes and the increasing time-lag needed to make any effective response. Both are enhanced, as well as relieved, by the increasing refinement of the tools which we are evolving to meet our needs. These seem to be blurring the division of function traditionally drawn between policy-making and planning by magnifying functions which fall between the two.

I choose as an example the report of the Buchanan committee (1963) which seems to me to mark a significant change in form and substance in the process of British policy-making.

This committee was asked 'to study the long-term development of roads and traffic in urban areas and their influence on the urban environment'. Their first response was to analyse and restructure the problem given to them, which very properly they turned inside out. Briefly, they said:

'Apart from through traffic, which forms a surprisingly small and tractable part of the problem, urban traffic consists of journeys which begin or end at urban buildings and which are generated by activities in those buildings. Thus the traffic is a function of the buildings. Even more clearly, urban roads are a function of the way urban buildings are arranged. Buildings in towns need the accessibility which is required by the activities which they generate. If these

96

activities clog the roads with traffic, the resultant mess is a symptom of a deeper problem, the problem of providing urban buildings with accessibility.

'This includes accessibility on foot, which conflicts with accessibility for vehicles. But even this is far too simple; for urban buildings need more than accessibility. They need services, light, clean air, quiet, perhaps a pleasant outlook and other amenities. These demands (summarized as environment) are not fully compatible with each other or with accessibility. The problem is so to design towns that their buildings may enjoy that combination of accessibility and good environment which is deemed to be the best; and to enjoy it as fully as can be achieved with the resources available. What resources shall be made available and what priority shall be given to these conflicting demands – these are for the policy-maker, not the planner. But until the policy-maker has thus restructured his problem, he cannot make these decisions and until he does so, he cannot instruct his planners.'

This, then, is the first of the committee's contributions; but they make two more. They suggest and explain new ways by which these disparate goods can be combined far more effectively than traditional ways allow. Streets still serve all the purposes which they have served since medieval times – through traffic, delivery and removal of goods, personal journeys on foot and by vehicle to workplace, shop, and school, social visiting, perambulation, gossip, and, now, parking. The multi-purpose street is as out of date as the medieval great hall; and its capacity can be similarly increased by sub-dividing it for specialized purposes. This can be done horizontally or vertically or even by allotting different times to different uses. A town must be planned as a whole and in four dimensions if it is to provide an optimum combination of all the conflicting uses which we want it to serve.

Even so, conflict will remain. How can the bewildered policy-maker know which of the plans offered to him best combines the priorities implicit in his sense of values? Again the committee come to his aid with yet a third contribution; a system of 'cost-benefit' analysis which claims to translate the achievement of

97

different plans in the disparate domains of accessibility and environment into comparable figures, representing value for money.

None of this, perhaps, is planning; but it is work which planners are best fitted to do. Significantly, the report is the work of a departmental study group. An independent 'steering group' commented on the report and drew some conclusions for public policy; but it was not responsible for the report itself. It seems reasonable then to regard the report as typical of the contributions which experts are expected to make to the circular process by which policy is made.

This help comes in all the three main areas of the policy-maker's task – in defining his problem; in conceiving the terms in which it is soluble; and in comparing the relative importance of the always conflicting values inherent in any solution. For all this the policy-maker may be duly thankful. But three questions suggest themselves.

First, why does he need these aids? He needs them because all three aspects of his proper task now require of him innovation to an unusual degree. The urban environment, once self-limited by breeding pestilence, is now limiting itself by breeding more activity than it can contain. To enlarge its capacity for containing activity by planning it continuously in four dimensions is a novel and a mammoth task. It must be simplified by selecting those aspects which shall receive attention – and those which shall be ignored. This act of abstraction, unavoidable even in simple situations, becomes far more important and more difficult, as the situation becomes more novel and more complex. It needs the co-operation of specialists.

The second aspect of his task depends even more on innovation by other minds. New ways of doing, even ways not yet achieved, excite the relevant professions long before most laymen have heard of them. The policy-maker is no longer conscious of the terms in which his problem might be solved. He must turn to specialists. (In the context of the Buchanan report he must turn not only to town planners but also to innovators in the fields of institutions and public finance.)

The third aspect of his task is equally beset by the need for innovation, which is equally unlikely to occur to his unaided mind. Any of his traditional valuations may prove to have become out-dated without his knowledge. Buildings can eliminate noise, fumes, and dust by sealing and air-conditioning. Conceivably, whole neighbourhoods might be isolated within artificial climates. Is the value of the open window as outmoded as the open fire? Who can tell, until he has worked out the cost in other amenities which is involved in clinging to this one? Techniques for this kind of calculus are still rudimentary but they are already fields of growing technical skill and they are being widened with the obsessive devotion which in our day only technology commands.

So the answer to the policy-maker's first question is, I think, that he needs these aids because in all his traditional functions he is called on to innovate in a way which makes him dependent on the expert.

The second question arises from the first. Does this mean that the real role of policy-making is increasingly passing to the expert? And must the policy-maker become an expert or a rubber stamp? The answer to both questions I think, is 'yes'. Big business has already met the same challenge. The business policy-maker needs more than a nodding acquaintance with system analysis and system design. Tomorrow, the man trained in these techniques will have impressive qualifications to succeed to the policy-maker's seat. The implications for our political institutions form part of the doubts from which I began.

A third, more radical, question underlies the other two. What are the dangers of these new techniques? Can we ensure that the benefits will outweigh the costs? To this question I will return. I want first to widen the field of attention, by referring to some other examples.

II

The State of California recently contracted for the making of four studies similar in character to the Buchanan report but more varied in scope. The subjects for inquiry were crime and delinquency; government information; transportation; and 'waste management'. The contracting parties were the Space General Corporation; the Lockheed Missile and Space Company; North American Aviation; and Aero-Jet General Corporation. None of these corporations had any previous experience of the subjects entrusted to them. They had, however, distinguished themselves in designing systems for defence or space exploration. In American government and big business the analysis and design of systems has already become a science and a profession applicable to any field which is important enough to warrant the attention of these rare and expensive skills.

The immediate history of this development is well known. When Mr Macnamara became Secretary of State for Defense, he took over the still unaccomplished task of welding the armed services into one; and he brought with him from industry concepts and methods of operational research which were admirably suited to show, in objective and quantified ways, the shortcomings of service-departmental schemes, when judged by defence-departmental criteria. In August 1965, the President of the United States directed that all non-defence departments and agencies of the Federal government should adopt and apply so far as possible the methods developed in the department of defence, which have become known under the deceptively narrow name of programme budgeting. The Rand Corporation produced a clear and modest statement of these methods (Novick, 1964), significantly avoiding the assumption that they would prove applicable in all non-defence fields. Time has yet to show their uses and limitations.

This development is the confluence of several streams. Operational research, born in the mass production industries, grew in strength and diversity during the war, in response to the need to find new or better ways to achieve specifiable aims, industrial and military, old and new, and to test them effectively before becoming committed to them. The design of weapon systems and warning systems and space exploration systems since the war has given ever greater scope for the art. The development of computers has supplied an essential tool. The study of system theory has enlarged the relevant conceptual framework. Communication science has developed mathematical models and techniques. All this has greatly improved our capacity to deal with problems which cannot be solved by trial and error, because such trials would be too expensive or too slow or would change the situation too much.

Political problems and the traditional ways of solving them clearly need to be scanned with the fresh eye which operational research, as now conceived, can bring them. Political problems, even more than industrial or military ones, do not lend themselves to solution by trial and error, since such errors, apart from being too costly and too slow in showing their effects, change the situation in which they are tried and leave new problems in their place. So the politician, even more than the director of an industrial corporation or a space exploration programme, should welcome any development which will help to simulate the situation in which, on various hypotheses, he will be acting and to evaluate the effects on that situation which hypothetical, alternative plans might have.

His problems, however, are different at least in degree from those to which the methods of system analysis and system design have usually been applied. The criteria of success for any political action are multiple and conflicting, as the Buchanan example has shown. They cannot be compared in importance or even identified, until the situation which involves them has been analysed by a circular process which may involve several circuits. Traffic congestion suggests at first no more than inadequate roads. The inquiry 'what would be adequate?' reveals a mutually exciting relation between roads and traffic and shifts the inquiry to questions of accessibility and thence to 'good environment', changing at every step the situation involved and multiplying the values to be considered. The more fully the situation is explored, the harder becomes the task of striking a balance between its multiple and disparate needs. So the policy-maker should scan with hopeful attention any help which his new-style planners can offer him in reducing these disparate values even partly to comparable figures on a common scale.

But these gifts are ambiguous. Some of the present values of programme-budgeting are indeed manifest. It is clearly useful to budget policies, irrespective of the agencies which carry them out, and to budget them over a period of years long enough to disclose both their benefits and their costs. It is useful to budget their benefits in terms of the policy which they exist to further, even where these benefits cannot be defined in quantitative terms; for example, when they can only be described as degrees of accessibility or environment. It is useful to budget them in terms of total resources required to achieve the policy, rather than of present commitments alone. It is useful, in comparing disparate values, to know what difference it would make to direct a given quantum of resources here rather than there. The policy-maker who looks askance at the limitations which remain when these have been allowed will not easily explain why his unaided limitations do not alarm him even more.

Yet sufficient doubts remain to raise the question which I deferred earlier. Does not the application of these techniques to political decisions bring threats, as well as promises?

Exponents of the system would regard the answer as self-evident. Their argument is clear and cogent. They might put it like this:

'The circular process you have described is not new; it has only become more difficult. We offer techniques which may help you. How far they can help only time can show; but at least they cannot hinder. Our analytic techniques do not claim to tell you where your analysis should stop. Our budgeting techniques do not claim to tell you what values to assign to the variables involved; but they do tell you far more clearly than you could discover for yourselves what would be the effect of different possible valuations. They can expand your achievement to the limit of your capacity for valuation. They cannot do more; but without them you will certainly do less. By making your values explicit, you are more likely to give them the weight you mean them to have than if you allow them to work or be forgotten in the comfortable obscurity of your unconscious mind. And if you multiply these disparate elements so far as to defeat us, our rational process will at least carry you further than your unaided judgement would have done.

'For your judgement is necessarily full of arbitrary decisions. The results of your proposed actions overflow into every field of policy and echo indefinitely down the corridors of the future. You must in any case decide what to notice, what to ignore, and where to stop the calculus of cause and effect. If we make you take these decisions and make these assumptions rationally and explicitly, are they not more likely to be right and will you not be the wiser for knowing more clearly what you have omitted and what you have assumed?'

It is a cogent argument but it can be challenged, thus:

'Powerful new tools always change the processes to which they are introduced. In time the entire activity is modified to suit what the new tools can and cannot do. This has been the history of industrial technology and it will surely be the history of technology applied to the political process. It is therefore proper to ask what the new servant will do to the master and the master's purposes. We may be sure that the answer is not fully predictable but the dangers are apparent.

'First, there is a dilemma inherent in the programme-budgeting process. It begins, as the Rand memorandum puts it, with "structuring the problem"; and this, as we have seen, may mean transforming it. The essence of this transformation is to reveal the numerous and disparate values which have to be accommodated.

But it ends with budgeting costs and benefits; and this grows less realistic, when costs and benefits have to be reckoned in terms of a multi-valued policy. So the better the problem is analysed, the harder it is to budget alternative solutions. This is likely to give the analyst a vested interest in shaping problems to the capacity of his budgeting techniques; and this will reinforce the policy-maker's natural reluctance to wrestle with the infinitely difficult and wearing task of multi-valued choice.

'It will further weight the scales in favour of what can be specified and measured – or even made to look as if it had been specified and measured – to the exclusion of what cannot be specified and measured, and so reinforce the always formidable pressures which tend to exclude such factors. It will thus increase the rigidity of the policy-making process, burying assumptions even more deeply than they are buried now; and so it will restrict what it is most expected to increase, the capacity for innovation. For the voice of the innovator will have to battle not only with the human voices of tradition but with the voice of the new authority, the programmed representation of what is, the programmed forecast of what will be. The resistance with which he has always battled will be shifted to a level even more inaccessible than before.'

This suspicious plea for human intuition may derive some scientific reinforcement from the following argument. The new techniques depend increasingly on the power of the digital computer. There is no doubt that human brains function in part as digital computers; and in so far as they do, these tools vastly improve an essential function of the human mind. But there is evidence (admirably summarized in Dreyfus, 1965) for believing that human brains also use analogue techniques, which we have at present no machines to simulate; and these powers are essential to the most important achievements of the human mind, notably the creation and recognition of significant form which underlies good judgement in politics, no less than in ethics and art and, conspicuously, science. The danger is that the new techniques, while aiding our less important mental powers, will block or even mask the existence of those which are far more important.

It is hard for the non-expert to know how much substance there is in these fears. It is significant that some of the experts share them (see Boguslaw, 1965, esp. p. 185). Dr Carl Stover (1966), on the other hand, president of the Institute for Public Affairs in the USA, in an appreciation of the California experiments, writes:

'Systems approaches, to be used well, require careful thought about the goals we pursue and the conditions for achieving them. At the same time, by permitting us to understand better total problems in their full context, they also make us more thoughtful. To ensure so felicitous an outcome places special burdens upon public officers, from highest elected officials to citizen. If we embrace systems techniques, our politics must become more sophisticated or our systems analysts may become our most sophisticated politicians.'

It places also a special burden on the analyst, to identify and constantly re-check, rather than bury and forget, the assumptions, the omissions, and the valuations which are built into his model. And among the burdens of the policy-maker there will still remain the need and the duty sometimes to take decisions in conditions of complete uncertainty. We may even arrive at a new and welcome definition of uncertainty, as a state in which different but equally probable assumptions, put into the computer, yield opposite results. But this would assume that policy-makers and system analysts continue to hold the same idea of what, in politics, constitutes sophistication. And this, unhappily, is not to be assumed.

In any case, the value of the argument is chiefly to alert both layman and expert to the fact that there is something to argue about. For the new techniques will be speeded not only by the passion of the technologists concerned but also by the fact that, however crude their methods may still be, they help to correct the rival crudities implicit in the traditional yardsticks of economics. As an economist recently observed (Lowe, 1965), the subject-matter of classical economics is the study of markets. It is both ill adapted and unaccustomed to measure either benefits or costs accruing to anyone other than the parties to a market transaction. Social benefits and social cost have in consequence been ignored or concealed, with consequences that grow increasingly calamitous as political choice replaces market choice as the arbiter of the things that matter most.

A new link in London's underground transport, for example, obviously distributes benefit not only to its users but to all the users of surface transport, which moves faster in consequence. For more than thirty years the public undertaking which controlled public transport both on and under the surface of the city, pooled the costs and equalized the fares, despite the vastly greater capitalization of the underground work. Yet it is a recent and daring innovation to include among the benefits of a new line a estimate of the value accruing to surface transport, irrespective of the parties to whom it accrues.

The Buchanan report supplies a further example of our current confusion, when it is compared with the Robbins report which appeared almost at the same time. The Robbins report on higher education devotes a whole section to arguing that money spent on higher education should be regarded as an investment rather than a cost, since it will produce a return in economic, as well as other, terms, although none can calculate its money value or predict where its benefits will fall. The Buchanan committee, on the other hand, though dealing with the development of real estate, treats capital expenditure not as investment but as cost and makes no reference to the enhanced value of land and buildings which will result from redevelopment. Nor in its comparative cost-benefit analyses does it suggest that one might show a better money return than another.

Wherever these rival sciences of value-measurement are going, no one would want them to rest where they now are.

III

At the beginning of this paper I expressed two doubts. The first concerned the institutions needed to make any policy appropriate to our needs. The nature of these doubts has now appeared.

It has been a basic assumption of our political life that policy is made by elected policy-makers. There is debate about the changing roles of parliament and the executive; but there are only the first rumblings of debate about the distribution of power between elected government and its permanent staff. Any criticism of this is resented as if it could only imply a slur on the loyalty of the public service.

Yet if my analysis is right, the changing relations between the executive and the legislature are bound to be paralleled by changes in the relation of the executive and the machinery of government; for both proceed from the same cause. The regulative task of government has grown in scope and difficulty. It is concerned with every aspect of the national life. It involves the management, directly and indirectly, of immense operations. It must make assumptions and take commitments which extend far into the future. And it requires new skills, which these new tasks have called into being. Those who are responsible for these great tasks, if they are to influence them without wrecking them, need to be as closely associated with them and as well equipped to control them as are those who manage great industrial empires. Here a similar change has taken place. Not long ago, part-time directors, the 'elected' representatives of the shareholder-owners, were deemed capable of controlling the policy of businesses, which were supposed to be efficiently run for them by their servants. Today, most directors of businesses are their whole-time employees, while of those who are not, nearly all have long experience in other businesses.

Policy-making is a collective enterprise, ever more dependent on the continuous processing and appraisal of information by the staffs of those on whom rests formal responsibility for decision. I have already suggested that these today must be experts if they are not to be wreckers or rubber stamps. The expertise is of a new kind but it involves no less long and arduous learning than older and more familiar specialisms.

This expertise is scarce. In the USA its largest field of development is the mammoth corporations which have grown up in the private sector, though those which serve the public sector are becoming increasingly dependent on it and ever less distinguishable from it (for a good summary, see Weidenbaum, 1966). This expertise is at the disposal of governments through the simple mechanism of contract, as the California examples show. More important, outstanding individuals are equally available to fill the highest executive positions in the federal government, except the presidency, since with that exception none require political election. The governments of fifty States and several super-cities further extend the training-ground, as well as the demand. In Britain the training-ground is far smaller and the shape of her political institutions makes it far harder for governments to draw on outstanding individuals, except as advisers. Yet here as in USA the need grows for highly competent chief executives at the heads of departments of State. Here, as there, 'public officers, from highest elected officials to citizen' need to be capable of politics at least as 'sophisticated' as their advisers.

My second doubt can be more briefly stated. Let us suppose that our policy-making institutions are or become such that they can generate policies equal to our needs. This will often mean, equal to our children's needs; for few important policies today can become effective until ten, twenty, or even thirty years after the date when the search for them first begins. We often disguise this from ourselves by ignoring logistical limitations, especially those of skilled manpower, which depends not only on the length of vocational training but on countless individual choices of career made years before under the influence of elders speaking from a yet older past. Any realistic policy must be able to count on the human, as well as the material, resources needed for its execution.

What kind of electorate, what kind of party system would make it possible for any government to come to power on a programme made of such long-term and presently expensive policies; or for any series of governments to carry them out?

The question needs, I think, to be put in a longer perspective. The great protagonist of operational research in government was clearly Jeremy Bentham. To test the utility of legislation by its proved or calculated ability to contribute to policy, this was surely in the spirit of programme-budgeting. Nor has there been much overt change in the overriding principle which he proposed as a criterion of policy. Nearly two hundred years have passed since, as a young man, he read in a pamphlet of Joseph Priestley the statement that the aim of life should be the greatest happiness of the greatest number. Yet few today would overtly question this general principle, even though few in any generation have pursued it with the enthusiasm which it awakened in Bentham.

A weird historical accident identified his creed with an individualism which had its roots elsewhere and led first to legislation designed to sweep away laws which appeared restrictive of individual freedom and to extend political power not to the greatest number but to those whom Bentham thought would speak most intelligently for them. But in principle his creed was as apt to support a socialist, even a communist, polity as to bolster the individualism which was its first beneficiary; and its identification with individualism has been assailed and eroded ever more strongly and successfully from his day to ours.

The middle third of the nineteenth century was marked by legislation designed to release individual energies. Its most potent step, perhaps, was the first Companies Act, which enabled private citizens to found at will profit-making corporations capable of accumulating property indefinitely – a right which until then had been a jealously guarded privilege. The middle third of the twentieth century has been marked by legislation designed to release collective energies and to curb the powers and enforce the public responsibilities of great corporations grown in a century from the seedbed laid down a century before. All parties still profess, at least in principle, the utilitarian criterion; but how far does our mass democracy agree either on the conditions of its happiness or on the identity of that 'greatest number' for whom it is supposed to plan?

Daniel Bell (1960), heralding the end of ideology insists that 'the present belongs to the living' and warns us that the future, no less than the past may lay a dead hand on the present. The present does indeed belong to the living but only as trust property belongs to trustees, even where the trustees are tenants for life. The greatest number are, we hope, the unborn; but even among the living the greatest number, in most countries today, are the young, still preparing for the world that their elders are making for them. Bentham's criterion can no longer be wrapped in the grave-clothes of *laissez-faire*. It stands out, as in principle it always has, to maintain the claim of others against self, of tomorrow against today, of the weak against the strong, of the poor (nations, now, as well as individuals) against the rich. For the first time we have at last to face its *costs*.

So perhaps it is apt that there should appear at the same time the programme-budgeter, with his cost-benefit analysis and his innocent, obedient air. 'What values, sir, shall I insert here? And here? And here? Would you like to know what difference a little more patience, a little more altruism would make? Just a moment, while we reset the computer.'

Dr Stover is right. To make democracy work in the world and on the time-scale of today 'special burdens' must be carried, not only by 'highest elected officials' but by citizens also. These burdens have no place at present in the political philosophy of Western nations. It is time they were acknowledged and taken up.

Maybe the programme-budgeter can help.

This paper originated as a presentation to a discussion group at the University of Keele, England, in 1967, and was published in the Political Quarterly, *July–September 1967.*

REFERENCES

BELL, D. 1960. *The End of Ideology.* New York: The Free Press.

BOGUSLAW, R. 1965. *The New Utopians.* Englewood Cliffs, NJ: Prentice-Hall.

BUCHANAN, C. 1963. *Traffic in Towns.* Report of the Steering Group and Working Group appointed by the Minister of Transport. London: HMSO.

DREYFUS, H. L. 1965. *Alchemy and Artificial Intelligence.* Available from the Rand Corporation.

LOWE, A. 1965. *On Economic Knowledge.* New York: Harper & Row.

NOVICK, D. (ed.). 1964. Program Budgeting. Washington: US Government Printing Office.

STOVER, C. F. 1966. The California Experiment – An Appraisal. Available from the National Institute of Public Affairs, Washington, D.C.

WEIDENBAUM, M. L. 1966. The Effects of Government Contracting on Private Enterprise. *George Washington Law Review,* Vol. 15, No. 2.

·6·

The Multi-valued Choice

I am a lawyer and administrator. Such knowledge as I have of the psycho-social sciences on the one hand and the sciences of communication and control on the other has been gathered in the search for concepts, models, and theories with which to explain and understand the doings which have occupied my life. Those now available are not sufficient for the job, so far as I can see; but they are far more adequate than they were even twenty years ago. In particular, I have been impressed by the enlargement which communication theory has already brought to the psychological models of human motivation.

The focus of my concern is the multi-valued choice. I will explain what I mean by this, why I find it obscure and intriguing, and what conclusions I have tentatively drawn about it. I hope these will be clearer, sounder, and more adequate when we have finished our discussion of them.

II

The clearest example of the multi-valued choice is the settlement by a national government of its budget. I have argued elsewhere (Vickers, 1965, Chs. 10, 11, 12) that this is only a specially clear example of an ubiquitous experience, that every choice is in some measure multi-valued. However this may be, many of our most important choices are clearly multi-valued in the sense I shall describe.

The government is responsible for maintaining through time a number of relations with the world outside its frontiers; notably its balance of payments, the external value of its currency, the furtherance of its foreign policy, and the maintenance of its security. Equally it is responsible for maintaining a number of internal relations, such as full employment, public order, public health, the standard of living, and a host of others. All these are ongoing relations; and in each case there exists in the country and in the minds of members of the government ideas of what these relations should be, which serve as standards by which to judge what is and what might be.

These standards are usually latent in the mind, ready to arise whenever some concrete situation evokes them. A security scandal reveals that security arrangements are not as good as they were supposed to be and thereby reveals the standard which had previously been regarded as both requisite and good enough. Alternatively, an account of education or public health in some foreign country invites the view that the standard by which the corresponding domestic arrangements had hitherto been judged satisfactory ought to be raised or changed. Every discussion of policy involves the comparison of what is or might be with some standard of what is acceptable; and it generally results not only in some action to reduce the disparity but in some change in the standard itself.

Sometimes the only way to reduce the disparity is to change the standard. For these latent standards are often partly contradictory or unattainable with the resources available or even prove, with experience, to be less satisfactory than they were thought to be. Government involves constant adjustment both of the way things are going, to bring them more into line with the relevant standards, and of the standards, either to accommodate them more nearly to what is attainable or to bring them more nearly into line with new levels of aspiration.

What I have described will, I think, be recognized as familiar not only in the government of a country but also in the regulation of an individual life and it seems likely that the two processes are the same in character. The essence of my concern is the process by which these sets of standards are generated, co-ordinated, and changed, whether in public or private life, and the part played in that process by human communication. For we should not spend so much time in committees, board meetings, legislative sessions, and so on if we did not believe that talking to each other made a difference, not only by communicating facts but also by changing each other's standards – including our own – of what is important and how it should be evaluated.

The relations which the government has to maintain – and hence the standards which it has to set – are both external and internal. This is, of course, true of the regulator of any other dynamic system, be it General Motors or Kansas City or the drug-store at the corner or the man who keeps the drug-store. Each of these is a complex organization, which hangs together only so long as it maintains its essential internal relations; and it is these which enable it to act as a whole in maintaining all those relations with its milieu on which it equally depends. A predator's hunting depends on its digestion; and equally its digestion depends on its hunting. An organization depends similarly on renewing itself by constantly taking in from its milieu materials, money, and men, to balance consumption and wastage, no less than on the ways in which these are organized within it. Viewed thus, any organization may be seen as appropriating and using materials, money, and men, as a cow appropriates and uses grass, air, and water. So I will call these relations metabolic relations.

This, of course, is not the only way in which these organizations view themselves and are viewed by those within them and those without. They have a host of functions to perform and a corresponding set of standards by which to judge their performance. To return to the government in my example, it has not only to balance its budget but also to achieve, within that balanced budget, an optimal or at least an acceptable realization of the manifold things it is trying to do. Wildly disparate aims, such as atom bombs and medicare, highways and higher education, fight for realization, each an expression of the urge to bring some relation up to standard. No built-in hierarchy or order of priorities decides how far each shall have its way. The choice is multi-valued.

Even the metabolic choices are multi-valued. Only an act of judgement can decide over what period a budget need be balanced or at what level; revenue, as well as expenditure, is partly a function of policy and the time dimension has no limit save what our own choice or our own limitations impose. Nor can the budget be reduced to money alone; men, materials, time, skill, and (not least) attention all have their own limitations. The functional choices are even more multi-valued. For some functional relations are mutually inconsistent; and all compete for limited resources. The more abundant the life, the more multi-valued the choices are – and should be.

To sum up, then, the regulators of systems such as I have described are required constantly to perform a double process – a balancing process to keep in phase their metabolic relations and an optimizing (or, more exactly, in Herbert Simon's phrase (1957), a 'satisficing') process, to realize such a combination of functional relations as the regulator regards as optimal or 'good enough'. This process, which I will call the 'optimizing-balancing' process, involves the regulation of both internal and external relations; and, in this, metabolic and functional relations are inseparably linked; for they are different aspects of the same relations. Every winning or spending of resources also affects some functional relation. Money in and out is the metabolic side of the coin; service (or disservice) rendered or received is the other.

I want to stress three aspects of this model. First, such a system, if not deliberately regulated, will regulate itself after a fashion. The flow of money out will in the end have to conform to the flow of money in. Inconsistent policies will mutually frustrate each other. The sole aim and justification of policy-making is to impose on the flux of events some pattern more desirable or less repugnant than it would otherwise take. Thus all policy-making assumes that the policy-maker possesses or can evolve standards by which to judge the desirable and the repugnant; assumes, in other words, that he is able to value. Every policy-maker, merely by playing the role, warrants his own belief in his capacity for multi-valued choice; and all debate about policy similarly implies belief in the power of human communication to change the values of the participants.

Secondly, the recognition of policy-making as the regulation of *relations* stresses that the standards by which these relations are judged are not goals to be attained once for all but, like the mariner's course, must constantly be sought anew. I will call them norms. I have argued elsewhere (Vickers, 1965, pp. 31–34) that human regulative behaviour cannot be reduced to goal-seeking without masking the essential element which makes it different from the behaviour of rats in mazes.

Thirdly, the model describes regulation as *seeking* to attain or maintain some standard, rather than as *avoiding* some unacceptable threshold. It thus follows the custom of subsuming the negative under the positive. I adopt this reluctantly, because I believe that most regulative behaviour is negative, the avoidance of some relation which has been defined as unacceptable. Even the most positive aspirations of governments may be so regarded. The welfare legislation of my own country is based on a report which identified 'five giant evils'. The whole of human progress may be convincingly described as successive redefinings of the unacceptable.

It is still common, at least in my country, to distinguish organizations for public service from these operating for private profit by pretending that the former measure their success solely by the service they render, that is by functional standards, while the latter measure theirs by the money they make, that is by their metabolic standards. Both, of course, must have some regard to both aspects of their relations; for one must survive *in order to* serve, while the other must serve *in order to* survive. But for the one (so the myth runs) survival and growth are only the conditions, service the criterion of success, while for the other, survival and growth are the criterion, service only the condition. This simple dichotomy does not correspond with my personal experience in regulating different kinds of undertaking and I believe it to be false. Every organization, as I believe, uses both metabolic and functional standards of success, and the more it grows and prospers, the more complex and exacting become the functional standards by which it judges its own performance and is judged by others. I have found the same to be true of individual life. The multi-valued choice is a central, inescapable, irreducible fact of life.

It is equally clear that the standards by which these multi-valued choices are made continually grow and change. Look back a few decades over the life of an individual, a business, or a government; you will see that its standards of success, even the fields in which it is trying to achieve success, have changed. Governments have spawned new departments and agencies to deal with new problems – of health or poverty or housing or what you will; and these, like the older departments, have already developed aspirations and anxieties – standards of success and failure – different from those which governed them even a few years before. So have you and I.

Whence came these standards and changes of standard? They have clearly, I think, been learned by a kind of learning which has not yet been explored or even clearly identified. I believe that the theory of communication and control can help to identify and explain this learning; and that it needs to do so, since so much communication is devoted to it.

III

A simple control mechanism, such as an automatic pilot, exemplifies a cyclical, regulative process in three phases. Information is received from the compass; it is compared with the course; and action (or inaction) is selected in response to a signal generated by the comparison. The effect of the action (mixed with all the other influences which have affected the ship's course in the meantime) is fed back in the later intake of information and contributes to selection in later regulative cycles. Anticipation cuts down the time-lag but introduces hazards which I will not explore now. I will label these phases 'information', 'valuation', and 'action', and I will sometimes refer to them as the first, second, and third phase or sector of the regulative cycle.

The third phase depends on combining the first and second; for only when the 'right' information about what is happening is compared with the 'right' standard about what ought to be happening is the signal generated, which moves the selector to choose the 'right' response.

The automatic pilot does not usually have to learn how to carry out any of these phases. It is simpler to build in the appropriate readinesses to notice and to respond and to feed in the course from a source outside the system. It would be possible to devise an assembly which, given the right signals and the course, could learn – empirically or by calculation – the right rudder movements to select; could learn, in other words, the best solution to the problem posed by the third phase, the phase of action. It would also be possible, though more difficult, to devise a system which, though flooded with information of all kinds, could learn to systematize it and select from it what was relevant for holding a course; could learn, in other words, the best solution to the problem posed by the first phase, the phase of information. Both these possibilities, however, depend on the presence of the criterion of success supplied by the second phase.

Could we devise a system which could learn to set its own course? Clearly yes, if we could specify how to calculate the answer. A great circle course, for example, involves frequent changes in the actual setting of the course to be steered; the calculation of these changes could easily be transferred from the brain of the navigator to a calculating machine. But the great circle course itself had to be chosen. Why sail *that* great circle course? Why go to Baltimore rather than to Buenos Aires? Why go anywhere? We seem to be involved in an infinite regress, leading sooner or later to a choice made by applying a process which cannot yet be specified to data which remain obscure.

Learning in the second phase evidently presents some curious problems.

Now let us turn to the other end of the scale, to the regulation of human life in all its complexity. The individual at birth, let alone conception, is almost without sensory discrimination and therefore almost sealed to information. He has no power of co-ordinated response, beyond a few reflexes and thus has most limited capacity for action; and he has no 'criteria' beyond a few unco-ordinated impulses. Twenty years later he moves at ease in a conceptual world of great complexity; he possesses a large set of readinesses to respond to very varied situations; and he regulates both his input of information and his output of behaviour according to an elaborate set of criteria. Clearly, a lot of learning has taken place in all the three sectors I labelled information, valuation, and action, learning which is still in progress, though its future course in each of these three dimensions is increasingly governed by its past.

If we extend our view to take in all the societies, cultures, and sub-cultures in which he participates, we shall find that each of these also is characterized by its current state of organization in each of these three dimensions – by the kinds of information it is ready to notice, the kinds of valuation it is ready to make, and the kinds of action it is ready to take. These also are not static; they have grown and changed noticeably, perhaps dramatically, in the same twenty years. And between their growth and the corresponding growth in each of their human participants there has been constant, mutual interaction.

We do not, I think, distinguish sufficiently between these three different kinds of learning. The one we know most about is learning in the third phase – learning how to do. We know more about this partly because it is sufficiently developed in other creatures to be studied in them in the laboratory and the field and partly because, whether in animals or men, its results are more easily identified and measured.

Maze-running rats are indeed only rudimentary discoverers of the best way to do things, when we compare them with the livelier members of, say, a Du Pont research and development team. The mental processes by which humans solve problems of 'how to do it' need study at a higher level than the laboratory of the animal experimenter; and this study they are now receiving, through the alliance of psychology and computer science. Professor Simon, in a recent book (1965), declares his belief that whatever the human brain can do in this direction will soon be within the power of the computer.

Learning in the first sector is somewhat different, because the criteria of success are different. It is also more obscure, because its results are not directly or immediately apparent. There is, however, no possible doubt that it takes place, because the whole of science is its product and its monument. Science, as distinct from technology, is devoted to developing a coherent and comprehensive way to represent and understand the world we live in and call reality. The criteria for deciding the rightness or wrongness of the solution to problems in this sector are different from those which decide the rightness or wrongness of the solution to technological problems. Philosophers of science debate, still inconclusively, the claims of rival criteria and the nature of the knowledge gained. Experimental psychologists can help them even less than they can help students of technological learning, though they can distinguish, in non-human creatures, some learned knowledge of 'what is', as distinct from knowledge of 'how to do'. It appears in particular in an animal's knowledge of the topography of its home ground.

Learning in the second sector, the learning of criteria or standards of success, though least studied and least understood, is no less obvious and no less different. It is also the most important (in so far as any one element in a cyclical process can be given such predominance); for it sets the problems which the whole regulative process has to solve. That it is obvious I have already sought to show. That it is different appears from the fact that it appeals to criteria different from those which confirm or disprove learning in the other two sectors. How, for example, can the advocates of 'more money for education' (and, by implication, less money for something else) *prove* that their valuation is right and their opponents' valuation is wrong? How are such issues decided at all? Yet the facts are that they are decided; that great effort is spent on the advocacy which is supposed to affect their decision; that this advocacy has an observable pattern; and that this pattern has clear similarities to and differences from the pattern of debate which leads to decision in the other two sectors. If we cannot observe the process of learning, we can at least observe the process of would-be teaching. And this, I suggest, generates questions, if not answers, which are important both for psychology and for communication science.

IV

The second phase is the field least illuminated by either of these sciences. I have no space to summarize all the findings which seem to me relevant. So I will try simply to describe what seem to me to be the three characteristic procedures in the advocacy of value.

One of these procedures is to define the relation to be judged as being within some category to which the value advocated already attaches. A crime, for example, has long been regarded as a disturbance of the social order (demanding correction) and as a disturbance of the moral order (demanding expiation); but it may also be regarded as a protest or a cry for help by a distressed individual. Those who think that the criminal law, in some instances, unduly sacrifices the criminal to the supposed good of society, usually begin their advocacy of a change by insisting on the validity of this way of 'seeing' crime, a way which does not invalidate other ways but which should not be invalidated by them. Once seen as a symptom of distress, the crime attaches to the criminal the same claim to compassion and help which attaches to other individuals in distress, especially if the distress can be subsumed under the narrower category of 'illness', or 'handicap', to which an even more specific valuation attaches.

This procedure is familiar in 'first-phase' learning also and serves to stress the interdependence of information and valuation. We notice only those aspects of reality which 'interest' us; we have language to describe only those aspects which interest us. Interest is the basic fact of mental life – and the most elementary act of valuation. Thus the information which we seek or accept and the ways in which we organize it are largely determined by our interests in it. Predators soon learn to notice whatever is relevant to catching their prey. Humans collect and retain whatever information is relevant to the more varied and enduring interests which distinguish them from other creatures; and their enhanced powers of collecting and organizing information in turn quicken their interests. The elaboration of the reality system and the value system proceed together. Facts are relevant only to some standard of value; values are applicable only to some configuration of fact. I have suggested elsewhere (Vickers, 1965, esp. pp. 39–40 and Ch. 4) that the word 'appreciation' be used for those combined judgements of fact and value which we constantly make and I have compared our systematic readinesses to notice and to value, to the weft and warp of a net.

All the psycho-social sciences, especially child psychology and social anthropology, have shown that mental life and hence personal and social regulation are based on the development of schemata for classifying experience. The schemata for classifying sensory, especially visual, experience have been the most fully explored but there seems to be no room for doubt that all our experience is similarly classified by schemata, which are constantly changed and enlarged by use, as a filing system is changed and enlarged in response to the changing volume and content of the input.

The multi-valued choice always involves different ways of *seeing* the same situation, ways to which different values are attached. Like the ambiguous figures drawn by psychologists, it can be validly seen according to any of its schemata, even all in succession; but only in one way at a time.

To multiply the schemata relevant to the same situation greatly burdens the deciding mind and is always resisted. Advocates of valuations attached to schemata which have thus been subordinated have first to establish the claim of such schemata to apply to the matter in hand. It is worthy of note, I think, both to psychologists and to communication theorists, that what is involved here is the question whether a specific event should be accepted as within a specific category. It involves a process of 'matching'.

As such, it depends on the processes of first-phase learning. For example, it is well-established psychological theory today that some kinds of psychological deprivation in childhood make more likely some kinds of delinquency in later life. This theory of causal relationship supports the claim to assimilate the delinquent to the same category as sufferers from other handicaps in youth. It also more subtly undermines its assimilation to the category of crime, since this is entangled with a theory of responsibility which takes no adequate account of 'handicap'.

The next process is directed to increasing the importance of the value attached to the new schema by the deciding mind. This process, though most familiar, is still obscure. The advocate displays the event in the light of the schema by which he wishes it to be judged; he declares his own valuation; and he invites others to share it. He says in effect – 'Do you really not find this desirable? Do you really not find that unacceptable?' Those whom he seeks to persuade appear to be perfectly free to reply – 'No, we don't'; and if they so reply, he has no argument wherewith to *prove* them wrong. Yet this form of advocacy is potent to increase the weight attached to the value advocated, in comparison with the weight of other values involved.

It is significant, I think, both to psychology and to communication theory, that in this procedure, unlike the previous one, the appropriate metaphor seems to be weighing, rather than matching. Weighing is a dynamic concept; it involves the comparison of forces. Matching is an informational concept; it involves the comparison of forms. Both are involved in the 'teaching-learning' process by which values are developed; and though they are closely related, I think they should be carefully distinguished both by psychologists exploring the process of multi-valued choice and by communication theorists attempting to model it.

A third procedure needs to be distinguished. The advocate of a valuation may set out to create a new schema, corresponding to the new value. This is in fact one of the commonest facts of experience, though few such advocates have achieved enough to become personally identified with the change. The example I have given depends on the existence, in our societies, of a peculiar valuation of the individual human being, as having some rights merely by virtue of his humanity and these rights equal to those of any other man. This valuation is in fact accorded only partially and discontinuously in any society and to most different degrees in different societies. In societies where it exists, it has manifestly grown within quite recent times; and it has grown partly by the kinds of advocacy I have described.

These advocates have not been solely or even chiefly moral or religious leaders. They have been policy-makers, in government, in business, in the professions, wherever policy is made. For policy-making, as I insisted earlier, is not merely a balancing but an optimizing-balancing function; and the policy-maker is and should be a valuer, a setter of those norms by which optimizing, no less than balancing is measured, and potent as an advocate to secure the acceptance of the norms he sets.

For simplicity I have described this form of communication in terms of advocacy; but an advocate cannot wholly insulate himself against the replies which he elicits and he does not always wish to do so. The most effective processes of 'teaching-learning' in this, as in other phases of regulation, take place when every participant keeps himself open to influence by the others. I will describe these conditions as those of dialogue. We greatly need to understand them better, for they are most important and, even in the imperfect form in which we usually know them, they account for most of the learning we achieve in the second sector. The members of a policy-making body in which these conditions were wholly absent might still be able to drive a bargain with each other, but they would never reach an accord and they would learn very little from each other in the process, at least in the field of valuation.

There is, of course, a large body of theory about the origin of value judgements, from Marx, who saw them as rationalizations of economic self-interest, to Freud, who saw them as derivatives of instinctual drives. Marx and Freud mightily cleared the ground. Freud not only shed light on pathological motivation but posed the question of normal motivation in its appropriate form – 'How – and at what cost – do humans learn to regulate their individual and collective lives in ways so remote from those which their bio-logical endowment would lead us to expect?' But the question so well posed has not yet been adequately answered. It is generally accepted, I believe, that the ego, in dealing with its three hard masters, develops ideas of its own; and these ideas seem to develop in partial autonomy, though also in intimate relationship with the parallel process by which the schemata of the reality system are developed and changed.

V

I would insist, then, lest it be forgotten, that one of the main objects and probably the main effect of the deafening flood of communication which marks our place and time is to modify the value system of the participants; that this exchange is the medium for a kind of learning which merits attention in its own right; and that it should not be forgotten in the surge of exploration which communication science has started in the field of learning.

I urge this for at least three reasons.

First, the multi-valued choice, though inherent in human development, is far more dominant in Western societies today than it has ever been anywhere. It may already be setting problems which are strictly insoluble in the time and with the means now available. Traditional societies had value systems which were more simple, and more stable. Most of mankind today live in societies which either are still traditional or have ceased to be so only within one generation. (I recently heard a French scientist who had spent the last fifteen years in an African ex-colony, say – 'Until a decade ago it was unthinkable that an African should take a personal decision.') What we in Western countries regard as human nature is the fruit of a peculiar and recent historical development. How much, for example, do we owe, for good and ill, to the Lutheran revolution, with its insistence on personal responsibility?

Secondly, the problems of multi-valued choice are posed today on the international stage far more intensely, as well as more widely than ever before, by the clash of cultures which they involve. A culture enshrines common patterns of valuation, even common solutions of multi-valued choices. These problems may be escaping increasingly even from cultural control within a single culture; but in the inter-cultural arena they lack even these elementary guide-lines.

Thirdly, there is, I believe, a real danger that the power which communication theory has brought to the solution of problems in the third sector, problems of what to do, may further obscure the solution, even the existence, of problems in the second sector, problems of what to want. Critical path analysis is fine, if you know whither your path is leading and exclude every desire except the desire to reach its end. But it is only subordinate, if your path is a tentative compromise in the maintenance of a bundle of partly inconsistent norms – which in fact is what it should be. As a subordinate, even in such a situation it might in theory be most valuable; for logically, it should leave us more free for what Norbert Wiener called the human use of human beings. Psychologically, its effect may well be the reverse. For it has never been easy to subordinate problems of know-how to problems of know-what; and it is likely to grow even more difficult, through this enhanced power – unless, in exploring learning, we can become enamoured of the most intriguing aspect of that fascinating theme – learning in the art of valuation.

I should perhaps add a word about the relevance of these ideas to a symposium devoted to communication theory; for I know that to many it will seem of only peripheral importance, even if it is valid.

The scientific study of communication began in the laboratories of engineers concerned with problems of transmission. They were busy with problems of channel capacity and signal-noise ratio. At first they could take the organization of sender and receiver almost for granted. When it had to be explored – as, for example, to discover the minimal redundancy needed to make a message comprehensible – it was explored for the sake of economic communication, rather than from interest in the receiver as such. Soon the engineers were themselves designing senders and receivers, as parts of technological systems; but usually also as solutions to technological problems, problems which would not be attempted if there were no hope of solving them.

The psychologist and the sociologist start from a very different stance. They have from the beginning been trying to deduce the organization of the black boxes representing sender and receiver, from their responses to communication. For them the promise of communication science lies in the light it may throw on these otherwise inaccessible patterns of organization, rather than in better communication.

The promise has already borne much fruit; but it has naturally thrown least light on those human functions which communication science has been least required to simulate. It has therefore tended to fortify, rather than to debunk, the comfortable illusion that human valuations are a derivative from data which, if not apparent, are at least there to be found. And this illusion is further fortified by the feeling – a hangover from an earlier scientific age – that no other view is consistent with the regularity of the natural order of which science affirms man to be a part.

It seems to me, on the contrary, that communication theory makes clear for the first time the learning process by which values are generated and its partial autonomy in the cyclical process of regulation and thus opens for serious discussion the most important and unique propensity of the human mind.

Let me in conclusion suggest some of the topics which I hope our discussion will illuminate.

First among these I would place the interpenetration of fact- and value-judgement. The normative process applies not only to setting what we commonly regard as norms. For even that basic discriminatory judgement – 'this is a that' is no mere finding of fact. It is a decision to assimilate some object of attention, carved out of the tissue of all that is available, to some category to which we have learned, rightly or wrongly, that it is convenient to assimilate such things. The category itself has been learned and this learning involved both discovery and invention. When we understand this process better, we shall, I think, be able to arrange such discriminations along a spectrum, according to the degree of invention which is present in each, as they range from 'this is a cow', through 'this is a contract' to 'this is a sin'.

I am impressed by the fundamental nature of this process. In so far as I can be regarded as human, it is because I was claimed at birth as a member by a communicative network, which programmed me for participation in itself. Such autonomy as I have developed is not a relic of some inherent individuality which has survived socialization but is itself a product of socialization, differentiated out, learned deliberately through social experience, mediated by communication. It is, incidentally, a quality which most cultures regard as undesirable. Our passion for personal responsibility is, I believe, peculiar to the cultural stream which we know as the Judaeo-Christian tradition and has been fortified by contributions from sources as disparate as Luther and Adam Smith.

The individual, reflecting on the process by which he was humanized, can use only those powers of appreciation with which the process itself has endowed him. Since the mind is thus part and product of the society which it seeks to understand and has only its own powers with which to think about itself, I would not expect it – or any system – to be able to make a complete representation of itself or of any system of which it is a constituent. The extent of the limitation under which we thus labour is not yet apparent either in theory or in practice.

I am impressed, next, by the power of the process for innovation, not only in moulding the single life but in mediating continuity through change down the generations. When my grandfather was a boy, nothing in England moved faster than a horse; the Prime Minister had just fought a duel; and the still unreformed House of Commons was debating whether to abolish slavery. I felt at home in my father's world and more or less at home in the world of my older children, so in some degree my experience comprehends three generations. Yet only three hundred generations ago the last ice age was still withdrawing its glaciers from the shores of Britain and quietly vacating the area in which our history might in time begin. Those three hundred generations cover the whole agricultural epoch; the last half of it covers the rise and fall of all the civilizations of recorded time.

I am concerned, next, with the limitations which must bound the capacity of this process to preserve continuity through time and change and so to set some upper limit to its capacity for adjustment. That some such limitation must exist is clear, I think, from what we know of systems generally; all must be limited in the rate at which they can adjust all their basic variables, without losing that coherence which enables them to hang together and to operate effectively on their surround. But to determine when and where these limitations will arise, how, if at all, to enlarge them, and, in any case, how to keep the rate of change within the critical limitations – these are matters of high practical concern, about which we do not yet know very much. Everyone in these days is haunted, I think, by the knowledge that limitations are inherent in our situation; that we do not know them; and that our way of living, over what is really an infinitely short period, has set loose self-exciting movements which, for all we know, may already have taken us past the point of no return on the way to some abyss.

So any discussion of systems mediated by human communication must be haunted by the difficulty of distinguishing between trends which are inherent in any such system and those which are inherent only in our present system and which may therefore, as yet, have had no time to emerge. To this extent the past is no sure guide to the future. Yet many would say that it is not too soon to see signs of anomie and alienation developing in the Western scene. The mere fact that these words should have come into common use in the last two or three generations is perhaps itself significant.

These crises in development, whether in the individual or in a society, are essentially crises in communication. They stem from the fact that communication can no longer mediate change at the rate or on the scale required by the kind of world which our new way of life has called into being. The resultant loss of shared and coherent standards and hence of human contact is the state which we call anomie in society and alienation in the individual. I have already pointed out that even the multi-valued choice, as I have described it in earlier sections of this paper, is itself a function of our culture and may well be setting us already problems which are strictly insoluble in the time and with the means now available.

But let us be clear in what this crisis of communication consists. We do not lack means of communication. On the contrary, we have so great a superabundance that the task of selecting, collating, storing, and retrieving outdistances our best efforts to keep pace with it. This, however, is not the crisis I have in mind, though it is indeed critical. I am concerned not with the means of communication but with the shared appreciative system which must interpret it and which alone gives information meaning. Professor MacKay has pointed out that information is an incomplete concept, developed by communication engineers who could legitimately assume that sender and receiver were linked by a common appreciative system and who were not concerned with the significance of what they transmitted in developing and changing the very system which gave it meaning. This, however, far more than the means of communication, is the heart of communication science and the heart of the current crisis in communication. For it is this which is in danger of losing its coherence and its continuity; and it is on this that we depend absolutely for our specifically human functioning.

It is very odd that we have no name for these states of readiness to discriminate and to evaluate which are both the product and the condition of human communication – unless, indeed, their name is 'mind'. Perhaps this good old word has become so contaminated by overtones, spiritual, philosophic, atomistic, and individualistic, that we shall have to consign it to the museum, with phlogiston and the rest; but if we do, we shall have to invent another. I call it an appreciative system, because these readinesses are organized systematically and enable us, in indissoluble association, to discriminate and to value – readinesses which are specific, limited and incomplete and open to change, yet without which we should be – and once were – unable to discriminate or to value anything at all.

This nameless faculty is fundamental to many human problems. It is fundamental to education; for every educator knows that his main job is to develop in his charges capacities for understanding which are not yet actual. He knows that somehow, by introducing a mind to what it does not understand, it may be brought to understand it and thus to become receptive to all kinds of information about it, which will further develop its capacity for understanding. And he knows that the development of this capacity for understanding is the real criterion of his success – even though it is far easier to test a mind's content than its capacity.

The concept is equally essential to our understanding of the democratic process, dependent as it is on communication within a common universe of discourse, which it is a main object of that communication to preserve and develop. This process must itself be changed by our realization of its nature. The old, blind, but honest battles of the ideologies must come to an end soon; they have weakened each other too much and we know too much about them all. By what will they be succeeded? It is easy to prophesy doom, far harder to discern a path which might transcend their differences. Yet, if there is such a path, it is most likely to be found through the study of communication.

This paper was originally presented at the Second International Symposium on Communication Theory and Research held at Excelsior Springs, Missouri, in March 1966 and published in the proceedings of that conference (Thayer, 1967).

REFERENCES

SIMON, H. A. 1957. *Administrative Behavior.* 2nd edn. New York: Macmillan.

SIMON, H. A. 1965. *The Shape of Automation.* New York: Harper & Row.

THAYER, L. (ed.). 1967. *Communication: Concepts and Perspectives.* Washington: Spartan Books.

VICKERS, G. 1965. *The Art of Judgment.* London: Chapman & Hall; New York: Basic Books.

Part Three

Beyond Descartes

·7·

Appreciative Behaviour

Information, communication, and control are concepts of growing importance, which are being widely applied in psychology and the social sciences. They make it possible to form a model of what I will call appreciative behaviour – a model rough and speculative but better, I think, than no model at all.

Most current theories of motivation were conceived before it was possible to distinguish energy flow from information flow with the clarity possible today. In consequence, energy concepts were stretched to breaking-point and beyond to cover situations where information concepts were needed. Confusion and unreal problems resulted. The apparent discrepancy between 'mental' and 'physical' work could be a problem, until it could be clearly seen as the disparity between the energy needed to work a control system and the energy which the working of that system might release – as, for example, between the energy needed to operate an automatic pilot and the energy released by its activity to turn the rudder of a great ship. The concept of tension reduction, apt enough to the physical relaxation of a creature which had just achieved the 'goal' of satisfying hunger or sex, was carried over in unconscious metaphor to describe the abatement of any mismatch signal. The concept of goal-seeking, apt enough as a model of behaviour in those situations in which effort leads through successful achievement to rest, was generalized as the standard model of human 'rational' behaviour, although most human regulative behaviour, as I shall try to show, is norm-seeking and, as such, cannot be resolved into goal-seeking, despite the common opinion to the contrary. Even the word, motivation, has an archaic ring, reminiscent of the days when minds seeking an explanation for a happening were wont to seek first for a 'mover' and ultimately for a 'prime mover'. 'Drive', with which some writers seem to identify motivation, has even stronger energetic connotations.

The language applied to man-made, self-controlled systems distinguishes sharply between the energetic and the informational components. There is an ongoing physical process, a ship at sea, a plant in operation, or what you will, which is capable of changing its state in response to signals. There is an ongoing informational process (equally physical), generating the signals to which the main system responds. The informational sub-system derives its signals essentially by comparing information about the state of the main system, including its relations with its surround (for example, the rate at which the ship is swinging or the rate at which the heat in a vat is rising), with standards or norms which have somehow been set as criteria for these variables. The disparity between the two generates a signal which triggers change in the main system, perhaps through the medium of a selective mechanism which chooses between a variety of possible changes.

This simple schema marks out three fields of inquiry, within which fall all the main questions to be asked by anyone trying either to design or to understand such a system. First, how does the control system derive its information about the state of the main system? Secondly, how does it derive the norms with which that state is to be compared? Thirdly, how does the signal thus generated cause the selection and initiation of change in the main system? These three areas are equally relevant as areas of inquiry into much of the activities of men and societies.

For, as energy systems, men, like other creatures, are active by definition. Their biological nature requires them to discharge, as well as to generate, energy at some rate within the range appropriate to their kind. Any question in the form – 'Why is he doing that?' is misleading unless both asker and answerer understand it in its proper form – 'Why is he doing that, *rather than something else?*' Psychologists and social scientists have to explain not behaving as such but the exceptional selectivity of human behaviour; and this is clearly due to the exceptional capacity of men for receiving, communicating, storing, and, above all, processing information. As energy systems, humans are sometimes and to some extent controlled, like the man-made systems of the engineer, by signals generated by a sub-system conveniently called the mind; and when they are so regarded, questions about the organization of the sub-system can be asked in uncanny isolation from questions about the dynamics of the system as a whole.

The first and second fields of inquiry – the observation of the 'actual' and its comparison with the 'norm' – are indissolubly connected and important in their own right. This combined process I call appreciation. The third field – the choice of action – is separable and may be irrelevant. Appreciation may or may not call for – and if it does, it may or may not evoke – action which may or may not abate an observed discrepancy, action which I will call regulative action. There may be no observed discrepancy; match signals, no less than mismatch signals, are important and, as I shall seek to show, informative. There may be nothing to be done. The selective mechanism for action may act at random or may be systematically wrong. Appreciative behaviour is distinguishable from regulative behaviour and needs to be so distinguished if we are to make sense of human activities, especially of those which are least illuminated by principles derived from the animal laboratory or the mental hospital. Statesmen, administrators, judges, executives, like ordinary citizens in their ordinary affairs, are often reminiscent of the rat in the maze and perhaps seldom free from symptoms known to psychiatry; but more sophisticated concepts are needed fully to explain their behaviour at its most effective – or the behaviour of the scientist, whose theories about them must be equally applicable to himself.

To clarify behaviour at this level need not invalidate other theories of motivation; for, as R. S. Peters (1957) has pointed out, we have no reason to assume that any one theory of motivation will account for all human behaviour. On the contrary, there is abundant evidence that humans have developed new regulative capacities, in addition to those they share with other creatures, and have great difficulty in reconciling the two. Indeed, there may well be not two but several types and levels of control fighting for power in a single individual in any given context.

Ever since psychology defined itself as the study of behaviour, the most characteristically human behaviour has presented peculiar difficulty; for it has manifestly depended for its explanation on 'unobservable' activities within the human head, which cannot be inferred either from observable input or from observable output. Some electors, for example, though by no means all, behave at election time in a way determined not merely by what has happened in the world since the last election but also by what has happened in their heads in the same time; and very little of the second can possibly be inferred from the first (input) because the total volume of the first is so vast and the selection therefrom which individual minds choose to notice is so limited and idiosyncratic. Still less can these 'unobservable' activities be inferred from the way the elector votes (output), because the range of behaviour open to him is so limited. He can vote for A or B – or possibly C – or spoil his voting paper or abstain – a choice almost as limited as that of a rat in a maze; and like the rat, even the moment when he must make his choice is decided for him. In so restricted a situation any choice might flow from any of a wide variety of appreciative judgements.

Our voter, in so far as he is behaving 'rationally' (and this is the strand in his behaviour with which I am concerned), will have made comparative appreciations of the parties which seek his support on a dual scale – his approval of their policies and his confidence in their abilities. Both will be derived from the past and projected into the future, in the highly selective context of his 'interests'. This complex operation (which I examine more fully in the next section with the aid of another example) can be analysed into judgements of fact about the 'state of the system', actual and hypothetical, past, present, and future, which I will call reality judgements and judgements of the significance of these facts to him and his society, which I will call value judgements – reality judgements and value judgements being the inseparable constituents of appreciation. If we knew how our voter derives and represents these highly selective reality judgements and how he derives the standards by which to complete his appreciation, we should know all we need to know about his 'motives' at this level – whatever other motives may also be at work.

Most psychological research has concentrated on problems concerned with the selection of action; and for this purpose has held constant and made certain the relevant reality and value judgements. If we want to know how a rat solves a problem, we must know for certain what problem it is trying to solve; so we make it hungry enough to ensure that finding food is its dominant problem. But most of the problems which humans try to solve are set by their own appreciative judgements and cannot be guessed without making assumptions about how reality judgements and value judgements are formed.

There is a vast body of such assumptions. Even a behaviourist, when he writes a book, hopes that it will influence not the overt behaviour of his readers but the way they 'appreciate' the subject-matter; and he addresses them as persuasively as he can in the light of half-conscious assumptions about the ways in which appreciative judgements grow, develop, and change. He knows that the development of 'ideas' in the individual head has a history distinct from the history of 'event', though linked to it by close mutual bonds; and if he did not know this, he would be a poor scientist. For the history of science and the biographies of scientists are outstanding examples of the way in which the history of event and the history of ideas proceed in partial autonomy, though in intimate relationship, each conditioning the other yet each growing according to its own logic and its own time-scale.

The assumptions which we make about this ubiquitous and

important matter of appreciative judgement seem to me to owe less than they might and should to such light as science could throw upon them. The concentration of study on behaviour which is observable in the sense in which stars and rats are observable, to the exclusion of such human behaviours as talking and thinking, is influenced by a supposed limitation of scientific method which, I suggest, is at least exaggerated. Talking, indeed, is receivable as a communication, rather than being simply 'observable'; and thinking is accessible only as the content of communication; but they are not on that account inaccessible to science or dispensable by it. Is it not a little illogical for a scientist to mistrust communication as evidence of what is going on in others and to expect others to rely on it as evidence of what is going on in himself?

II

The deliberations of a single mind are only accessible through reported introspection; but collective deliberations are more explicit. The agenda which accompany them are often accompanied by supporting papers, statistics, reports, forecasts, and so on. Discussions and conclusions are recorded more or less fully in minutes. With the aid of tapes and ciné-cameras, the record could in theory be expanded to cover all the overt behaviour which accompanies collective deliberation. This activity is familiar and ubiquitous. It occupies much of the time of all those committees which occupy scientists, no less than other men, as of cabinets and law courts, boards of directors and university senates. Something, I suggest, can be learned from the study of these activities. Among this great diversity of bodies, one is of particular interest, because in it the appreciative function is isolated. This is typified by Royal Commissions and similar bodies in Britain and other countries, to which problems are referred not for action but for consideration and report. I will take as an example the Royal Commission on capital punishment 1949–53, whose report in 505 pages is available for all to read, with its far more voluminous minutes of evidence. The proceedings of this Commission illustrate as well as any other the explicit processes of appreciative behaviour and have an additional interest from the psychological nature of the issue before it.

The Commission prefaces its report with a statement of what it has done, in words which should make a psychologist's imagination boggle.

> 'Our duty ... has been to look for means of confining the scope of [capital] punishment as narrowly as possible without impairing the efficacy attributed to it. We had ... to consider ... how far the scope of capital punishment ... is already restricted in practice and by what means; and whether those means are satisfactory as far as they go ... how far capital punishment has ... that special efficacy which it is commonly believed to have. We had ... to study the development of the law of murder and ... to consider whether certain forms of homicide should be taken out of that category and to what extent the liability ... might be restricted on account of ... youth or sex or ... provocation ... the extent to which insanity ... should ... negative or diminish criminal responsibility ... whether murder should be redefined ... whether any defects ... could be better remedied by giving either the judge or the jury a discretionary power ...'

and so on; leading to the conclusion:

> 'we thought it right to report at some length ... in the belief that, *irrespective of our recommendation* (my italics), it would be useful ... to place on record a comprehensive and dispassionate picture of the whole subject ...'

The nature of appreciative judgement could not be better illustrated or defined.

By far the greater part of the report is devoted to describing all relevant aspects of the situation as it is and as it might be, by applying to a great variety of fact and opinion, partly conflicting, the selective, critical, and integrating mental activity which I have called reality judgement. This is interspersed with comments expressing the commissioners' own approval or disapproval, their value judgements. Each section ends with recommendations for action, with regulative judgements.

The reality judgement is voluminous and complex. What homicides fall within the legal definition of murder? What kind and degree of insanity exclude the offence, what kind and degree of provocation reduce it to manslaughter? How varied are the motives and circumstances attending these crimes and the personalities of those who commit them? What is the purpose and what the effect of death or any punishment in such diverse cases? What are the respective roles of prosecutor, judge, jury, and Home Secretary in deciding which of those convicted shall hang? To these and many other questions answers are offered, definite or tentative, with whatever historical background is needed to make the present explicable.

The report has a double story to tell; the story of the relevant events and the story of the relevant ideas; and it moves easily, unconsciously between the two. The numbers and details of murders committed, of convictions, reprieves, executions belong to the world of event. The attitudes of men to murder and to the death penalty, the interaction of these two in giving murder a special status among crimes, these belong to the world of ideas, a world no less susceptible of factual report. Between the two worlds is an infinity of subtle, mutual connections which the commissioners must disentangle as best they may; for these interactions lie at the heart of the problems committed to them. What is, what should be, the relation between criminal responsibility as a legal fact, defined by the common law; responsibility as a medical fact, defined, they are assured, by the criminal's neural organization at the time and thus no less factual than the law but assessable only by the often divergent judgements of psychiatrists; and responsibility as a normative judgement passed by men on men, a standard of what *should be deemed to be* the scope and limits of their responsibility, yet a standard not without effect on the actual state of minds which know they are to be judged by it?

Based though it is on the present and the past, the reality judgement is concerned primarily with the future, which alone can be affected by any change now made. The death penalty could be limited by changing the definition of the offence or by subdividing it into 'degrees' or by admitting a discretion as to sentence. The reality judgement must arrive at an assessment of the probable effect of these alternatives, collecting what evidence seems relevant about the experience of other countries which have abolished, relaxed, or reinstated the death penalty; and about the problems attending the long-term custody of prisoners convicted of crimes of violence.

Some of this evidence is significant in at least two ways. The commissioners, having collected the views of police officers on whether abatement of the death penalty will increase violent resistance to arrest, must evaluate these statements of opinion both as evidence of what is likely to happen in the world of event and as evidence of what is actually happening in the world of ideas. For the apprehension of the police about the effect of a change in the law, whether well or ill founded, is both a fact and a force in the present situation and one which may indirectly alter the effect which such a change will actually have – for example, the willingness of police officers in Britain to continue to work unarmed.

The evidence on which the commissioners found their reality judgement varies vastly in certainty and in character. Statistics and estimates; opinions, often discordant, on matters both of fact and of value; the views of different authorities, past and present, on the legitimate purposes of punishment; the views of psychiatrists on human responsibility and its impairment by mental illness; all this and more goes into the mill and out comes the reality judgement, balanced, coherent, urbane, a mental artifact which only familiarity robs of the wonder which is its due.

The report is also sprinkled with the commissioners' own value judgements – usually expressed as agreement with value judgements found as a fact to exist in the community but none the less their own. Insanity *should be* a defence to murder. The then existing rules defining insanity for this purpose were narrower than they *should be*. Among the sane who are convicted of murder, culpability varies so much that they *should not* all be sentenced to the uniform, extreme, and irreversible penalty of death. The abatement of this penalty *should not* be left to so great an extent to the Home Secretary. It *should not* be left to the judge; or (for different reasons) to the jury. It *should* be expressed in the law itself. In these and a dozen other contexts, the commissioners, going beyond the recording of other people's value judgements, commit themselves to value judgements of their own. Whence came the norms which produced these value judgements?

The answer is simple but subtle. The commissioners used the norms which they brought with them to the conference table; but these norms were changed and developed by the very process of applying them; by the impact of the reality judgement which they focused; by the impact, attrition, and stimulus of each commissioner on the others; and by the exercise of their own minds as they applied them in one way and another, on one hypothesis after another, in the search for a better 'fit'. As an illustration, consider their debate on the use of the Home Secretary's power of reprieve.

It was their value judgement that, among people convicted of murder, culpability varied so much that punishment should also be variable. This, they realized, could be achieved (within their terms of reference) only by elaborating the definition of the crime or by giving someone discretion to vary the penalty to suit the facts. The first alternative they found in practice to be immensely difficult. The second was already in operation, in that nearly half those convicted of murder were reprieved on the recommendation of the Home Secretary. Was it 'satisfactory' or even 'proper' that so large a discretion should be vested in the Home Secretary? Eminent witnesses were divided. To make the Home Secretary 'an additional court of appeal, sitting in private, judging on the record only and giving no reason for his decision', said some, 'does not fit into the constitutional framework of this country'. The Arch-bishop of Canterbury objected on different grounds: ' ... it is intolerable that this solemn and deeply significant procedure should be enacted again and again, when in almost half the cases the consequence will not follow ... a mere empty formula is a degradation of the law and dangerous to society.' Other distin-guished witnesses found it not at all intolerable. Lord Samuel suggested that 'to maintain a degree of uncertainty as to what would happen in marginal cases may be very useful in retaining a deterrent effect on potential criminals'.

The commissioners' appreciative judgement was that the Home Secretary's discretion was 'undue'; but the only less objectionable alternative seemed to them still too repugnant to recommend. So their appreciative conclusions on the point were expressed without any recommendation for regulative action. Such recommenda-tions as they did make, they admitted, 'would go very little way towards solving our general problem' (i.e. how to relieve the executive of this undue responsibility). They concluded that 'if capital punishment is to be retained and at the same time the defects of the existing law are to be eliminated ... the only practicable way of achieving this object is to give discretion to the jury to find extenuating circumstances requiring a lesser sentence to be substituted'.

This appreciation, though without a recommendation and indeed all the more on that account, is perhaps the most important part of the report; for it amounts to a finding that there was no satisfactory half-way house between the existing state of affairs and the *abolition* of the death penalty. Their terms of reference precluded them from recommending or even considering abolition; yet a major contribution of their report to the appreciative judgement of their contemporaries was to support the movement for abolition which had in fact occasioned their appointment.

The report made some recommendations for action. Some were adopted in the Homicide Act 1957; some were ignored. Yet if all had been ignored, the major importance of the report as an appreciative judgement would have remained the same. The state of the commissioners' minds on the subject of capital punishment, after they had made their appreciation, was different from what it was when they began; and this change, communicated through the report, provoked change, similar or dissimilar, in greater or less degree, in all it reached, from serious students to casual readers of newspaper paragraphs; and thus released into the stream of event and into the stream of ideas an addition to the countless forces by which both are moulded.

Yet their terms of reference, on the face of them, required them only to recommend means to a given end.

III

If words mean anything, the Commission's report attests a process which is as wide as history, yet endemic in each individual head. If we range over the doings of Britain's inhabitants for the last millennium, we see the course of event and the course of ideas unrolling, each impelled by its own momentum yet each influencing and being influenced by the other – the *entraînement des choses* which de Tocqueville found as a salient datum of history matched by an *entraînement des idées* which is inseparable from it but which cannot be resolved into it. If we narrow our observations to the development of a few individual lives, say the members of the Commission, we find the same duality. The attitudes of mind which they brought to the conference table were the fruit of this unending interaction of events and ideas in their individual lives; and the attitudes they took away were further changed, both by the event of the Commission (and other relevant events which happened while it sat) and by the mammoth exercise and exchange of ideas which it involved. Psychology may leave the wider study to the historians but it cannot disown responsibility for the narrower one.

I am proposing that we should regard this mental activity as a

specific form of behaviour, 'appreciative behaviour'; unobservable in the sense in which scientists observe the behaviour of stars
and rats but attested by and studiable through the whole volume
of human communication, not least the communications on which
scientists invite us to rely when they formulate theories about
stars and rats. This activity consists essentially in making what I
have called reality judgements on selected aspects of their surround
and evaluating these in terms of value, including 'interest', which
I shall distinguish. A man's capacity for appreciative judgement
can then be described as depending on (i) the quality of his
relevant mental faculties, which seem to vary widely between
individuals; (ii) the materials at his disposal, whether in memory
or externally accessible or derivable from these by further mental
process; and (iii) his current state of readiness to see and value
things in one way rather than another, which I will call his
appreciative setting. This setting is a product of past experiences
in appreciation and will be confirmed or further changed, however slightly, by the next exercise. In the space remaining I will
try to give these terms some more solid content.

Clearly, we must credit our kind with the capacity to classify
'objects of experience' – what that covers I will examine later –
according to categories, which give them meaning by relating
them to each other. In the field of perception this capacity has
been well explored. The child learns to see, building up by experience the schemata by which further experience may be classified; learning to recognize cows in all their variety by their
correspondence to some generalized schema in which 'cowish-
ness' has come to reside and by the same process amplifying,
refining, and sometimes revising the schema for future use. The
same process attends the learning of an adult skill; the medical
student cannot 'read' a pulmonary radiograph until experience of
many has built up the interpretative schema. The learned character of such schemata is revealed most dramatically by the painful
confusion of adults born blind who acquire sight first in later life.

Less work has been done on the development of concepts but a similar process is clearly involved. Indeed, concepts *are* schemata for classifying objects of attention of all kinds, perceptual schemata being one class among many. The growth of scientific theory is the best-documented example of the development of conceptual schemata.

The self-determining process by which schemata grow by their own exercise is of particular importance. The child cannot recognize a cow until it has built up a 'cow schema'; yet the schema can only arise from repeated experience of cows. G. H. Lewes well described this elusive process as long ago as 1879: ' . . . the new object presented to sense, or the new idea presented to thought must be *soluble in old experience,* be *re*cognised as like them, otherwise it will be unperceived, uncomprehended.'

The process is clearly seen in the growth of the common law. Negligence, for example, is a complex concept. It means such a lack of care as makes a man liable to those who suffer thereby; but this is a circular definition. How much lack of care brings an act within the category? The common law will not define this more precisely than by pointing to all those past cases in which negligence has been found to be present or absent. Every new decision leaves the existing schema reinforced or, however slightly, changed. It is by nature incomplete and incapable of being completed.

The mutual link between the use and the formulation of schemata – and equally between norm-setting and norm-seeking – is even clearer in an engaging legal abstraction called the reasonable man. How much care would a reasonable man take of his own property? In what circumstances would a reasonable man feel justified in defending himself with violence? The courts will tell you, never in general terms but in the specific circumstances of any particular case to which the standard is relevant. So the reasonable man remains perpetually young, changing his character from century to century, as custom and culture change, and playing a potent part in directing, speeding, or restraining the changes which he reflects. He came to the aid of the commissioners when they were debating what degree of provocation might abate a charge of murder.

It follows that the appreciative setting of an individual or a society must always be latent. It is not revealed even by the latest actual judgement; for the making of the judgement may have changed the setting of the system, as the commissioners changed their own settings and, in some measure, the setting of 'public opinion' by the judgements embodied in their report; and it will change further in the course of the next judgement which it guides. The dissolving of new experience in the accumulation of old experiences, to revert to Lewes's simile, does more than assimilate the new experience. It also modifies, however slightly, the 'solution' in which the next new experience must be dissolved.

It follows further that schemata, though readily developed, resist radical change. The medical student's teacher cannot help seeing in the radiograph what the student has not yet learned to see. This stability is bought at a price. Professor Selye (1956) has described how, as a medical student under instruction in the different syndromes characteristic of various diseases, he was at first far more impressed by something which his teachers ignored – the striking *similarities* in the conditions of illness from whatever cause. This naïve observation, suppressed at the time, recurred years later to be the prime mover in his studies of physiological stress. Every major development of scientific thought has been long resisted because of the disturbance which it brings to the coherence of existing ideas; and this resistance is well founded, for coherence is precious. The body of scientific thought, like an individual's understanding of his world, can ill afford periods of extended chaos. The revolutionary solution, whereby new schemata are developed in carefully contrived isolation from the past, though sometimes necessary, is difficult and expensive, whether in politics, science, or the individual life.

Within this limitation, the schemata on which reality judgements are based are in constant development under three main pressures – the pressure of event; the pressure of other men's schemata; and the pressure of their own internal requirements. Events call constantly for new appreciations of the 'situation'. Other people's communications reveal schemata which confirm or challenge our own. And, apart from both these, the inner inconsistencies and incompleteness of our own schemata call us constantly to revise them. These are the occasions for appreciative behaviour – signals, whether of match or mismatch which confirm or question at the same time as they reveal the current setting of our appreciative systems.

The subject-matter comprised in our schemata is diverse. Only a very small part of it is given by sensory experience, even to the limited extent to which we now regard any sensory experience as 'given'. Most of it is the product of operations performed by our own minds and the minds of others. Such is a scientific theory – or for that matter an unscientific theory, like the Nazi theory of the Aryan race. The capacity of the mind to provide itself with artifacts on which it can perform further operations is one very good reason why the word 'mental' is needed; and would be needed, even if we fully understood the working of the brain and CNS. Professor MacKay (1956) has shown that the production of such artifacts can in theory be extended indefinitely.

We can handle what seem to be very complex objects of attention. The commissioners found no difficulty in matching the activities of the Home Secretary and his advisers in the matter of reprieve for murder with 'the constitutional framework of this country' and finding that it 'does not fit'. In that case the relevant cues were relatively recognizable and few. The Home Secretary was intervening so often that he was behaving like an additional court of appeal. Once so classified, he was obviously a 'bad thing', for he was 'sitting in private, judging on the record only and giving no reason for his decision'; and a well-established norm ruled that this is not the way in which a court of appeal should behave. Moreover, he was a part of the executive; and another well-recognized norm ruled that a branch of the executive had no business to be playing the role of court of appeal. Yet if his interventions had been sufficiently infrequent to escape classification by the schema 'court of appeal', he would have remained an acceptable embodiment of the Crown's prerogative of mercy.

The animal ethologists have taught us how few and how simple may be the innate 'releasers' that trigger complex sequences of innate behaviour. It may be that our learned discriminations are basically simpler than we know. It should not be impossible to find out.

Clearly, the objects of our attention include relations extended in time. This we should expect; for organisms and organizations *are* relations extended in time. Their continuity depends on keeping the more essential of these relationships within critical limits. The need, for example, for a man or an organization to preserve a balance between money in and money out is similar in character to the need to preserve a balance between energy in and energy out; and failure, beyond a critical threshold, produces no less self-exciting disturbances. The relations which a man, an organization, a society is set to attain or preserve (and to escape and elude) are manifold, as the Commission's report shows. They are for the most part a product of the self-determining, appreciative process which we are examining. For the moment I am concerned only to point out that they are not goals to be attained once for all but ongoing relations, like a ship's course, which must be continuously maintained – relations which I call norms.

It is usually assumed that such norms, from the agent's point of view, can none the less be resolved into goals, as the maintenance of a rat's metabolism, equally a norm, can be resolved into periodic quests for food. This, I suggest, is not so. The record of the Commission – and of every deliberative body – shows it well able to represent to itself relations extended in time and to compare these with normative expectations, similarly extended; and the once-for-all connotations of goal-seeking make for confusion if they become attached to norm-holding. A man who wants to become Prime Minister may and probably does seek the satisfaction of being appointed to that office and he may properly regard the attainment of this as a goal; but it is to be hoped that he also looks forward to supporting the complex relations which attach to the role and which must be sustained as long as it is held.

I stress the importance of ongoing relations as objects of attention because they seem to be unduly ignored. The dominance of 'objects' over 'relations' in our conscious thinking has often been criticized, but it still conceals the fact that we do not seek or shun objects but relations with objects. No one wants an apple; he wants to eat it, sell it, paint it, perhaps just to admire it, in any case to relate to it in some way or other. The relation may sometimes be taken for granted; people who avoid tigers need not be pressed to say why. None the less, at the level of mental behaviour which I am considering, the distinction is usually important.

We have no idea how these mental feats are accomplished but they seem less odd than once they did. To scan and classify according to schemata, even to build up better schemata by scanning are in their simpler forms activities not beyond the compass of existing machines. The coding of information admits of more development than we can foresee. Analogue computers provide ways of comparing complex relations, sometimes in ways which are familiar to us all in such forms as the map and the graph; it may be significant that relations in space and time are so much more easily grasped when presented in graphical or mathematical form than when expressed in words. Perhaps the dominance of objects in our conscious thinking is a by-product of the structure of our verbal language, which in turn reflects the dominance of vision among the senses.[1]

In any case, in thinking of appreciative behaviour, we need not suppose that the mental models which underlie appreciative judgement consist of words or images, though it is hard for those with visual imagination not to depict our judgement of reality as

[1] Not all languages are similarly handicapped. L. L. Whyte (1962) writes: '... the Hopi and others appear to put the cognitive emphasis not on separable traces, representing isolable entities but on the actual process of experiencing.' He also quotes Whorf (1954) as authority for the proposition that 'the Hopi ... view reality as events rather than as matter'.

'the image', as Professor Boulding (1956) has done in his classic assault on the problem. We use, even consciously, more models than words and images can supply; and we have no reason to suppose that the mind is limited to those forms of representation of which we are conscious. Indeed, the contrary appears from the fact that some, if not all, of our activities in ordering experience and especially in grasping temporal and casual relations occur at least partly in states of abated consciousness, especially in sleep. The commissioners' judgement was formulated in a report which speaks from conscious mind to conscious mind but I have not inquired at what levels of consciousness the actual mental work was done and it is one of the merits of the approach which I am using that I need not do so. As Whyte (1962) has observed, ' . . . the antithesis conscious/unconscious may have exhausted its utility'. All I have assumed in this analysis is the absence of *pathology* attaching to either state.

There is pathology of the unconscious, resulting from the mechanism of repression. There is also a pathology of the conscious, which still awaits its Freud – the pathology of those who, trapped in 'consciousness', became perpetual observers even of themselves as agents and who are thus cut off from essential conditions both of effectiveness and of joy. The man free from both these diseases functions none the less in a variety of states of consciousness, which subserve his performance in ways we do not understand; nor need we wait to do so before we try to model the overall process which they combine to mediate. It may well be that the conscious operations of the mind, though essential, are the least central to the process of appreciation. Such at least is the impression left on my mind by some experience of highly skilled 'appreciators'.

IV

Appreciative behaviour involves making judgements of value, no less than judgements of reality; so a psychology of value is inseparable from a psychology of cognition. An adequate psychology of value, when it is formulated – and this, I believe, is a proper and feasible task for psychology – will cover far more ground than I am attempting now; but some of it may be illustrated from the deliberations of the Commission.

It is convenient first to separate judgements of 'importance–unimportance' from other kinds of value judgement. Objects of attention may be picked out as being important – or, alternatively, parts of the field may be scanned with particular care as being likely to contain matters of importance – without making any qualitative assumptions as to what their importance may prove to be. The commissioners no doubt tried to approach their task with an 'open mind'; but this did not hamper them in deciding what evidence would be relevant. I will describe judgements of importance–unimportance as judgements of interest. Interest is the selector. It must precede reality judgement, even though other kinds of value judgement may follow later.

Next, I will distinguish two values which are inherent in the appreciative process itself. The first is certainty–uncertainty of expectation. Humans, it seems, have grafted on to an age-old capacity for 'action-now' a much more recently developed capacity to appreciate the future. Stress, as well as power, comes from this enlargement of scope. Men maintain expectations of the future course of their manifold relations and constantly scan the unfolding present for confirmation or disproof. Confirmation, even of an unwelcome expectation, reassures the appreciator of the validity of his reality judgement and to this extent is positively valued. Disproof, on the other hand, erodes the structure of expectation and challenges the validity not only of the judgement but perhaps also of the processes by which the judgement was formed. Thus match, no less than mismatch, signals are significant in the appreciative process.[1] This is true of the interaction of men

---

[1] Some writers subsume 'match' under mismatch signals, but this usage seems to me to be open to objection almost as serious as the practice of subsuming 'threat-avoiding' under goal-seeking.

with their non-human environment but far more true of their dealings with each other, in which confirmation of expectation is more needed and more prized; so it becomes more important as the social element becomes ever more dominant in the human milieu. It explains much in human intercourse which would otherwise be obscure. Communications which appear to add nothing to the recipient's stock of information are not meaningless if they confirm his expectation of the other party. Such, for example, are most small talk, greeting, and ritual.

Our expectations of the behaviour of the non-human world are largely based on 'laws', scientific or roughly empirical, which it is observed to obey; but our expectations of our fellow-men are based on 'rules' which they are expected to observe, and human intercourse is based on knowing, if not sharing, the rules on which the other is acting. It is the argument of this paper that such rules govern appreciation as well as action; govern the way the situation is seen and valued, no less than the decision regarding what action (if any) is called for. Thus the horizon of confident expectation entertained by men of each other depends on the extent to which they understand, even if they do not share, each other's appreciative settings. The degree of this assurance is of value, irrespective of the contents of the rules themselves.

The second value inherent in the appreciative process is the value of 'coherence–incoherence' in the inner world of the appreciator. His schemata are interrelated; and though the schemata of everyday life may be less exactly articulated than the schemata of science, they too confirm each other by their coherence and proclaim inherent inconsistencies by nagging mismatch signals. The commissioners, seeking a repository for the discretion which they felt bound to lodge somewhere, found none where it could be placed without importing inconsistency into a complex, existing role.

It remains to consider those judgements of the Commission which cannot obviously be reduced to judgements of coherence–incoherence. I will call these judgements of fitness–unfitness. As we have seen, the problems of the Commission all stemmed from the fact that a change in the valuation of capital punishment as such had for some time been shouldering its way into the closely integrated system of values surrounding crime and punishment, producing new problems of 'coherence–incoherence' among the valuations which it disturbed. Whence came the change?

It came, I suggest, from a change either in the schemata used to classify reality or in the (not necessarily identical) schemata used for classifying value; or in both. To identify these changes is not, I think, an impossible task, though it is not to be attempted here. I will only add some comments on the relation between schemata of reality and schemata of value.

The simplest valuations are attitudes attached to schemata of reality. The kind of court of appeal which the commissioners could approve was defined by objective criteria of reality. This is very common. In consequence many, perhaps most, changes of valuation come simply from changes in classification. My duty to my neighbour shrinks and widens with my conception of who my neighbour is. My attitude to mental illness will change if I extend my schema of illness, with its value connotations, to include something which I had not previously recognized as illness.

Valuations, however, have also schemata of their own, not identifiable with schemata of reality, as the Commission found to its cost when it tried to subdivide murder in definable categories of 'reality', corresponding to degrees of 'culpability'. A fair deal is different from a fair fight, because the rules applicable to the two situations are different; but fairness, as meaning the keeping of recognized rules, is a schema in its own right, applicable to both situations and to many more. (If the illustration seems too old-fashioned to be valid, it will serve further to illustrate the fact that schemata may lose their meaning through decay.) Value schemata develop, like reality schemata, by use through the subtle, self-determining process already described. The criteria of value, like the criteria of reality, are always latent in the mind, waiting to guide and to be changed by the next exercise. The key to the problem of value lies in the further exploration of this self-determining, creative process.

There remains the key problem – how does the appreciative judgement settle conflicts of valuation? For such judgements usually involve choices between 'goods' and between 'evils'. Even this rough inquiry suggests that such conflicts are not settled by some predetermined 'rank-ordering' of norms and goals; for even where such priorities exist, the need to choose arises only in a concrete situation, as a choice between specific alternatives and cannot be separated from them. The commission's decision that it would be less unsatisfactory to extend the discretion of the jury than to continue to rely so largely on the discretion of the Home Secretary cannot be expressed, even in retrospect, as derived from a pre-existing 'rank-ordering' of norms or goals or principles, irrespective of the situation in which the judgement was actually made.

The example does not provide an adequate answer to this ancient question but it seems to me to make a useful contribution. The Commission's judgement would alter the schemata of reality and value of the commissioners and of all who would be influenced by their report; and the commissioners, in considering it, were conscious that it would have this impact on the world of ideas, no less than in the world of event. They were responsible artchitects in both worlds; and in both they had to consider the impact of their action on the total situation. We are accustomed to thinking of judgement as a matter of 'weighing' alternatives, a dynamic metaphor, suggesting the comparison of forces. I have tried to show that it also involves a process of 'matching', an informational metaphor, suggesting the comparison of forms. We need this second concept if we are to understand and describe the commissioners' efforts to minimize incoherence and unfitness in the total situation. Here surely is a field of critical importance which information concepts can help to clarify.

This paper was originally published in Acta Psychologica, *vol. XXI, no. 3, 1963.*

REFERENCES

BOULDING, K. 1956. *The Image*. Ann Arbor, Mich.: University of Michigan Press.

LEWES, G. H. 1879. *Problems of Life and Mind*. London: Trubner.

MACKAY, D. M. 1956. Towards an Information Flow Model of Human Behaviour. *British Journal of Psychology*, Vol. 47, Part 1.

PETERS, R. S. 1957. *The Concept of Motivation*. London: Routledge & Kegan Paul.

SELYE, H. 1956. *The Stress of Life*. New York: McGraw-Hill.

WHORF, B. L. 1954. Time, Space and Language. In Thompson, L. (ed.), *Culture in Crisis*. New York: Harper.

WHYTE, L. L. 1962. *The Unconscious before Freud*. New York: Basic Books; London: Tavistock Publications.

·8·

The Normative Process

I believe that the conceptual separation of information processes from energy processes, which has taken place in the last two decades, will prove as important as the changes in our concepts of matter and energy and of time and space, which marked the earlier decades of the century.

I believe that one important effect of this innovation in our thinking will be to deepen our understanding of social processes and especially of what I will call the normative process.

More generally, I believe that it will advance scientific epistemology and, in particular, the epistemology of science.

These are the three ideas which I will develop in this paper, so far as space permits.

You will see that my optimism is in an unusual direction. I hope not for greater efficiency in our problem-solving but for better understanding of our problem-setting – which I distinguish, though some others do not. And my optimism coexists with some pessimism in directions more usually welcomed. I do not anticipate that what I will comprehend under the general name of communication science will prove to be wholly a blessing; indeed, it is already, I think, proving restrictive.

But I would stress first its liberating aspects. It models machines which, though undoubtedly physical, embody processes other than those we are accustomed to regard as mechanical. And since machines are powerful to naturalize in our minds the principles which they embody, these machines are bound to have an impact on our thinking. It is a feature of these machines that they separate the regulative, form-giving element from the dynamic elements of the system; and this is something which has been lacking in the models used by psychology, as well as biology, in the past. They thus enable us to talk, with a precision hitherto lacking, not only about communication but about the mental organization of the participants which gives the communication meaning to them – an aspect of the matter which I think is more important and more neglected.

Further, these models disclose the key part played by standards of comparison (or norms, as I shall call them) in giving meaning to information and thus focus attention on the normative process by which these standards are set and changed. And since this is an obvious characteristic of human life, they enable us to state much more clearly some of the peculiar differences which distinguish human communication from that of other creatures.

Incidentally, they seem to me to dissolve the old mechanist-vitalist controversy and to restate it in a far more fruitful form.

For all these gifts we should be duly grateful. Indeed, we can only now recognize the conceptual difficulties under which biological and, even more, the psycho-social sciences have been working.

It is sometimes forgotten, though not, I hope, by social scientists, that science is a human activity; indeed, an outstandingly human activity, since many people today regard the scientist, rather than the philosopher, hero, or saint, as the proudest achievement of our species. It is also an outstanding social activity, for it consists in a body of knowledge, a set of principles, a language, and an ethic shared and passed on by a body of men who are the severe and only effective critics of each other and themselves. It depends on communication between scientists, no less than on observations of phenomena; and, before admitting new ideas, it inquires how congenial they will be to the existing conceptual system, no less anxiously than how well they will fit the facts. It is a closely articulated mental artifact, by means of which scientists communicate with one another and pursue their collective enterprise and its coherence through change is one of their prime and proper concerns.

In all this it is not unique. The same can be said in some degree of the participants in any common culture, professional, religious, national, or racial. But science is an example of peculiar interest, because it combines in a high degree the need for precision with the need to grow and change. Since growth and change in a conceptual system depend on concepts *not* being precise, science exemplifies better than most conceptual systems the difficulties of peaceful change.

To a science which built up its earliest concepts (and its prestige) from the study of inorganic matter, organic form and behaviour have always been a problem. Newtonian physics conceived a world of inert matter, pushed about by forces external to it. Its configuratʾons were thus the resultant of these pushes and pulls. This conceʟt seems inadequate to explain organic forms or organic behaviour. The course of a river through its catchment-area, even those changes which are due to the activity of the river itself, are explicable by the laws of mechanics. The development of a tadpole into a frog is not – at least without an act of faith; still less, the development of baby Isaac into Sir Isaac Newton.

Man-made machines helped to model the variety which structural design can give to energy; so biology since Descartes has used mechanical models, which became more useful with the advent of the steam engine, to model the conversion of fuel into mechanical energy. But none of them threw any adequate light on the form of biological structures or the pattern of biological activities – except to those who postulated a divine engineer.

None the less, it remained conventional to postulate forces to account for forms. When Driesch insisted that his divided sea-urchin embryos could not possibly complete themselves, each into a perfect specimen, unless they were guided to that unrealized end by something outside the mechanics of his day, he described his entelechy as a 'force' and placed it outside the natural order – thus accepting half the assumptions against which he was rebelling. It did not occur even to him to postulate that every cell in his mutilated embryos carried a blueprint of the uncompleted whole. (Heaven knows what they would have called him if he had!) Yet within a decade after physicists had made that very idea respectable, his biological successors claim to have identified the genetic code.

Of course, biology, exploring the homeostatic mechanisms of the body, soon developed a concept of regulation which could not be wholly explained by any known mechanism; and in studying the relations of organisms with their milieu and especially with each other it recognized that change and stability can be mediated by information. But this of itself throws no light on how the message is read; just as to determine the structure of the DNA molecule identifies but does not break the genetic code. It would seem that before ideas become powerfully fertile in the conceptual world of science, they need to be embodied either in a mathematical equation or in a physical analogue. And the two have different results.

The revolution in physics which has occurred since the days of Driesch has been largely achieved by mathematics, at the cost of abandoning all physical analogues; and it has left physics vastly extended but also vastly humbled, wholly unsure whether its extended knowledge of relations between its own observations allows it to infer anything at all about the natural order itself. The revolution of communication science is different; for although it includes a notable development of mathematical thinking, it is also marked by dramatic model-building in digital (if not yet in analogue) computers and their use in control devices of immense refinement and startling success.

It seems absurd to describe this revolution as the *discovery* that *inform*ation means what it says; that it can impart *form*. Didn't everybody know that already? What is science itself but a huge artifactual *form*, built of *inform*ation? Maybe – but the idea lacked a foothold in the scientific empire which it had created. It is a matter of no small importance that this foothold has now been supplied.

The discovery arose obliquely; for, as Professor MacKay has

pointed out, the first exponents of information theory were engineers concerned with problems of transmission, such as line capacity and signal–noise ratio. They could take the organization of sender and receiver for granted. Hence their apparent unconcern with meaning, as distinct from information. But soon communication engineers, devising controls for spacecraft and automatic factories, were having to design their own senders and receivers in a communication network and to furnish them with programmes, determining what they should notice, how they should evaluate it, and what they should do about it. They had thus distinguished the three main functions of any regulator, including the human mind in its regulative capacity; and they had become directly involved in problems of meaning.

It was a limited concern, still far from the contemporary human scene; for they were designing *slaves* to serve the purposes of human masters. Nothing could be more inconvenient than to endow these slaves with power to develop purposes of their own. So only the most advanced research assemblies have yet attempted to simulate this salient characteristic of humankind. None the less, a conceptual barrier has been breached. Here are dynamic systems, a rocket, an automatic factory, a ship at sea; and here within each and forming part of each, is a no less physical sub-system, designed to receive, even to seek communications with its milieu, to compare these with standards built in, communicated, or calculated; and, in the light of these communications and processes, to decide what to do. The form of the resulting activity will be dictated not by anything inherent in the energy source but by the still, small voice of the control mechanism, which will need no more energy than is needed to send a signal. The model is as much a 'machine' as the models of Descartes; but the concept of a machine has radically changed. No wonder the word has gone round the campus – 'There *is* a ghost in the machine. It's a mechanical ghost. We've made one.'

It is not, I think, so simple as that; but one result seems to me indisputable. Communication science is today providing models

163

of man and society which are in some respects more useful and more sophisticated than those of biology and ethology, sciences which are still limited and sometimes distorted by the conceptual fetters which the physicists have so suddenly slipped. The only scientists still at home in the new physical world are those para-scientists, the social scientists, who never accepted the fetters, because, unlike the psychologists, they could not have functioned at all if they had. So they remained active, if slightly disreputable, until this change of front legitimized their favourite concepts. I am not sure, for example, whether anyone could yet, even in theory, programme an artifact to learn a 'role' and act according to it; but the sociologist can now describe what is involved in learning a role in language far more acceptably 'scientific' than was at his disposal when he devised the concept – and, incidentally, far more exact.

II

The development of perfectly general concepts for describing a communication network, whether human or artifactual or mixed, is clearly of peculiar importance to sociology; but it is also of importance to science generally, because the lack of these concepts has caused confusion at other levels also. Some of it is so deeply built in, that it will take time and thought to eradicate.

The objects to which scientists have directed their attention, from atoms to stars, from amoebae to men, no less than the relations between these, have all proved to be events, rather than objects, interactions extended in time. More exactly, the object of attention has proved to be the interface between two sets of relations which are themselves related. Thus if the object of attention is an atom, we are led to explore both the way it hangs together and the way it interacts with other atoms, neither of which can be understood without the other. An atom is neither more nor less than this complex of actual and potential relations. You and I may be no more but we are certainly no less.

It has been the task of science to explain change and stability, regularity and variation, in these continuing events. Where, as with the atom, the event has one state sufficiently definable and enduring to earn a name, we think of it as an object. Where it has not, our inveterate tendency to objectify involves us in unreal problems of identity. These habits of thought may be partly inherent in our language. If we regarded events as a category more basic than objects – as I understand some languages do – we should save ourselves a lot of trouble. We should also be more nearly in accord with what we know about the way things are. We have never yet identified a particle so elementary that it just *is* and it seems most unlikely that we ever shall. For I understand that even the ones we know have somehow lost that supposedly basic attribute of identity, without losing the capacity for relatedness. It looks as if objects were abstractions from events and relations, rather than the constituents of which these are built.

So the subject-matter of science is a hierarchy of systems. The study of this hierarchy is beset by complexities, which increase along several dimensions with the higher organization of the events studied. One of the uses of communication theory is in helping to order this hierarchy.

Even at elementary levels, be it cell or even atom, the object of attention is a dynamic system, a configuration of forces. If it is an organic system – and often if it is not – it is an *open* system, exchanging matter and energy with its surround. The more highly developed such systems are, the more open they are and the more extensive is the net of mutual interdependence in which they are involved. But while everyone is familiar with the idea of dynamic systems open to energy exchange, we are so little accustomed to distinguishing openness to information that we have no word to describe it. Yet only openness to information makes possible the development of systems such as sociologists or even biologists study.

The hierarchy of forms which science studies is ordered in ways which have emerged successively in the history of our planet. A river and a candle flame are dynamic systems, maintaining themselves as forms more enduring than their constituents by the operation of mechanical laws alone. But organic forms, even very simple ones, rely on information to regulate their internal relations. Much later in the evolutionary sequence, they develop means of using information to regulate their external relations also. As external relations come to include an increasingly important component of social relations with others of the same species, *mutual* communication grows in importance as a regulator of individual and social life, even in non-human species. Human societies, with their enduring but changing cultures, are inconceivable except as communication networks. And even among these, the transition from stable, traditional cultures to our own changing and unstable ones is a long spectrum, which we urgently need to understand.

The capacity for mutual communication, through the medium of an enduring culture, attests the emergence of a new means of mediating change and a new medium in which change can be mediated; and thus a new field for scientific attention. Until the appearance of communication science, this field was curiously ignored – except, of course, by social scientists. Scientists who wrote books insisting on the comprehensiveness of the scientific world-view seldom noticed that their activity in writing, the effect which they hoped their words might have on readers and on the symbolic system which they and their readers shared, all this and the whole tissue of shared and communicated ideas which made them scientists, was wholly unexplained by the scientific system whose comprehensiveness they were proclaiming; that that system itself was indeed one among many symbolic constructs of the human mind.

The peculiar status of systems such as men and societies within the natural order deserves a separate name to distinguish them even from other biological systems which, though also open to information, have not been able to construct from it a shared conceptual milieu. I will call them 'appreciative systems'.

It does not follow that communication science will render the subject-matter of the psycho-social sciences more amenable to what the physical sciences have consecrated as the scientific method. For as an object of scientific attention, man would in any case be an interface of peculiar difficulty. Both the internal relations by which he hangs together, biologically and physically, and the external ones by which he interacts with his social and physical milieu are extremely complex. Both show irreversible and in some degree unique change with time; and are thus embedded in history, that bugbear of scientific method. The all-pervading influence of communication gives every event a double significance – even the most brutal use of force between men and societies is usually even more potent as a communication than as a dynamic operation. Finally, to confound the confusion, our understanding of both internal and external relations is affected by unacknowledged sources of information and insight, as well as error, which are open to us and inescapable by us because we happen to belong to the species.

None the less, the models of communication science, even at present, are useful, so far as they go. Sociologists have always taken for granted the emergence, through language and mutual communication, of an enduring social nexus capable of generating, revising, and transmitting norms of action and thought. But the models of individual man which psychology at present supplies are inadequate to support these assumptions – as the atomic model was, until recently, inadequate to support a theory of molecular coherence – and the models of communication science are a welcome addition. It is useful for the psychologist to view the infant not merely as a bundle of drives, about to wind their way through the constraints of society, but also as a potential unit in a communication network about to be programmed by the process which will claim him as a member. It is equally useful for the social scientist to analyse culture and institution in terms of a self-programming network. At both levels the approach helps to counteract the traditional view that the form and direction of human activity are to be explained by something inherent in the dynamic structure, rather than by a semi-autonomous regulative system, the appreciative system, to which the dynamic system is organized to respond.

It thus helps to validate the sociologist's assumption that, while 'human nature' has indeed a dynamic biological structure, it is not a biological datum. Biological evolution made humanization possible but what makes it actual, even today, is upbringing in a human society. The revolutionary, the prophet, and the martyr, no less than the most conformist defender of the Establishment, defines himself, by protest if not by acceptance, in terms of the society which made him human. This process not merely of human interaction but specifically of human intercommunication generates those norm complexes which regulate social and individual life, and we may be thankful that communication science has legitimized the study of them in their own right. For the normative process, that most conspicuous feature of human life, has been coyly shunned by psychology and even by sociology, because of its supposedly unscientific overtones.

III

The most conspicuous fact of individual and social human life is the emergence of the normative function. The individual at birth is almost sealed to information; he has scarcely any power of co-ordinated response; he has no criteria beyond a few unco-ordinated impulses. Twenty years later he moves at ease in a complex conceptual world; he possesses a set of readinesses for action apt to most varied situations; and he pursues a variety of interests and commitments, if not without conflict, at least without allowing them completely to frustrate each other. Clearly, a lot of learning – and teaching – has taken place in all three fields. If we extend our view to include all the cultures and sub-cultures in which he participates, we shall find that each of these also is distinguished by its state of organization in each of these three dimensions – discrimination, evaluation, and action – and may also have changed, perhaps dramatically, in the same twenty years.

The kind of learning which has been most studied is learning how to do. We pride ourselves on our pre-eminence in this and we do indeed manipulate the physical milieu much more ingeniously than rats. We pride ourselves almost equally on our skill in learning to know – in building a system of concepts capable of representing the milieu and simulating its manifold changes; and here we beat our fellow species even more dramatically. The whole of technology is a monument to our success in the first field, the whole of science to our success in the second. Yet both these realms of achievement are meaningful only in relation to standards which define the success of action, the relevance and importance of facts, even the truth of propositions. We are less willing to realize that this, the field of valuation, is also a field of learning – and teaching. Yet it is these standards which most distinguish our species.

The culture in which we grow up is intensely normative in all three dimensions. The simplest discrimination – 'This is a that' – (whether 'that' be a cow, a contract, or a sin) is no mere finding of fact but a judgement which carves something out of the field of attention and assimilates it to a category which has been generated by previous acts of the same kind. The simplest valuation – 'This should be thus' – is equally a judgement arrived at by comparing some object or event or course of events (real or imagined) with some standard which has become accepted as the appropriate norm. The simplest decision on action – 'In these circumstances this should be done' – is the selection of a response from a repertory by rules which determine what is suitable to what occasion. The categories by which we discriminate, the standards by which we value, the repertory of responses from which we select, and our rules for selection are all mental artifacts, evolved, learned, and taught by the cultural process and more or less peculiar to the culture which produces them. This process is a circular process, in which all these settings of the appreciative system are constantly being modified by their own exercise.

Communication science does not yet directly model this circular process by which we constantly programme and re-progamme each other; but it focuses attention on the problem and provides language for its discussion. The three dimensions which I have distinguished are the three familiar phases of any control process. It is the comparison of actual with norm which generates in thermostat or automatic pilot the signal which evokes the regulative response. However complex be the process which constructs its representation of the actual and selects the strategy of regulation, neither is either possible or meaningful except in relation to the norm, the setting which the system is trying to maintain.

Traditional societies could take their settings for granted. We cannot. We have learned that our own, whichever it may be, is neither unique nor given, that we live in one of many possible 'appreciative' worlds and that other societies, living in sharply different worlds, press on us on every side. We have learned how incoherent is our own culture – and theirs – and how rigidly this limits what we – and they – can collectively do. We are conscious of cultural change in two senses, both threatening. On the one hand, symptoms of anomie and alienation suggest that the rate of change may have become disruptive and calls for stabilizing devices which we lack. On the other hand, political aspirations and fears call for rates of change which we have at present no means to achieve.

These threatening 'imbalances' are not to be described solely in dynamic terms. Clamorous and inconsistent mismatch signals arise also in the semi-autonomous 'appreciative system'. The whole concept of dynamic balance, developed in regard to dynamic systems, needs reformulation to cover appreciative systems.

Dynamic balance is only half the story. The policy-maker is expected not merely to balance but to optimize, to achieve, within the limits of the practicable, some state chosen as most desirable or least repugnant. The mere existence of policy-making attests the will to impose on the flux of event some form other than that which the interplay of forces would give it. Whatever scientists, as scientists, may say, men as political animals expect from their policy-makers – at least in our present society – not merely balance but artistry; the realization of social form, in redesigning cities, in enfranchizing minorities, in many not necessarily consistent ways. These demand consensus focused and sustained for decades – enduring settings of our appreciative system – if they are ever to be reflected in changes in the actual state of the milieu.

No human society has ever achieved these things, even in much more favourable conditions. We have no reason to believe that ours, new, untried, unstable as they are, can do so. But being set to try, we need to know urgently just those things about men and societies which we have hitherto been least well equipped to explore. Today, I think, thanks to communication science, we can ask our questions in terms much more likely to evoke useful answers. Whether they will be the answers we want is another question.

If we survey the contemporary mess with these thoughts in mind, we shall see, I think, exactly what we should expect to see in a world which knows a lot about matter and energy but very little about information and much less about meaning. For one should never lose sight of the fact that information is an incomplete concept. Whether it informs and, if so, what meaning it conveys, depends on the organization of the participants in the network in which it is used; and this organization is in turn developed by participation in the network.

It is an eloquent comment on our present stage of development that we have no generally recognized word to describe this state of mental organization which I am calling a setting. We have indeed much conventional widsom about it – in education, in politics, in advertising, in literature, including the literature of science, where authors, like other authors, adjust their words to the supposed settings of their readers' appreciative systems. But we have no word which would readily convey to the ordinary educated man what I am including in this still unfamiliar concept.

Or do we lack a word, not because the concept is unfamiliar but because it is a focus of anxiety and fear? Nearly every word which suggests its manipulation, from brain-washing to propaganda, is highly pejorative. Commercial advertising, political persuasion, even proselytism are at best ambivalent. Education escapes only by clinging to the deluding image of an influence which enables but does not *shape*. We do not *want* to know what sets and changes our settings – though we never tire of surveys to see how they are currently set and currently changing. We are almost equally nervous about seeking to understand the settings of other societies.

Such defensive reactions often guard areas which methodical inquiry is beginning to illumine; but they are strongest and best founded in this central citadel, where to know is itself to change.

IV

Against this background I would like to discuss several themes which I have barely time to mention.

I would like first to discuss the factors which in our day have made so dominant problems of competing ideology, whether in politics or economics or social relations, and have thus demanded so imperiously a better knowledge of what I have called appreciative systems.

Clearly, these are in part ecological. For at least half a million years our kind spread thinly over the planet, hunting and food gathering. Within the last ten thousand years, one-fiftieth of its total span, it adopted a settled way of life, based on agriculture and husbandry, and embodied in traditional societies those relatively stable patterns of relationship which have ruled most of the world until now. Within the last two hundred years, one-fiftieth of one-fiftieth of its span, a mere half-dozen generations, there emerged in a few Western countries and most explosively in the rich and empty North American continent an industrial way of life which has scattered its ideas and some of its techniques across the planet and set moving exponentially a dozen critical variables. Viewed as an ecological niche, the world is filling up as never before; and this further stimulates the technological explosion which was its cause. The important aspect of this from a sociological viewpoint is, of course, its linked demands for political innovation and cultural change, themselves amplified by the millennial hopes which the changes engender.

It is easy to show that the responses required involve the collective action of large populations, sustained over decades. A review of what has happened even since the Second World War shows how radical and how diverse are the responses of different countries to this challenge, different not merely between communist and non-communist States but within each of these vague groupings. Yet it seems obvious to me that the political and cultural changes required will be far greater than spontaneous adjustment will achieve.

But here we need from the social sciences some outline of the principles governing what I will call the ecology of the conceptual world; for the conceptual world has a life of its own. 'Like the life forms of the physical world, the dreams of men spread and colonize their inner world, clash, excite, modify, and destroy each other or preserve their stability by making strange accommodations with their rivals.' Every field of activity, politics, law, and not least science, like every society, has its own stability to guard. All communication – and hence all co-operation – depends on shared appreciative systems, on ways of conceptualizing and valuing which are systematically organized and which, when they change, may have to change extensively before they reach anything approaching a new equilibrium. I have already referred to the need to develop concepts of stability applicable to appreciative systems.

Within this field is one especially relevant to America and

Britain. The concept of individual freedom and responsibility, as we know it, is the product of a particular stream of Western history. It is not universal. Its significance in our own countries is changing. The early immigrants who settled in America, seeking, among other things, freedom of conscience, had an idea of conscience different from yours or mine. Those who fought for *individual* freedom from arbitrary executive power had not experienced the *social* responsibility that success would bring. Our concepts of freedom, of the private sector, of the relation between public and private power, are all on the move.

These, I think, are only a few of the reasons why competing ideologies, within as well as outside national frontiers, are of such public concern today. It is they which determine what possibilities, if any, are open to government – national, international, or even intra-national – to realize any of its aspirations or even to maintain a viable society. And we know little more about them than did our great-grandfathers.

The aspirations of a society are not given by biological evolution. That doughty exponent of evolution at the end of last century, T. H. Huxley, said in a famous lecture – ' . . . the evolution of society is, in fact, a process of an essentially different character from that which brings about the evolution of species . . .' and later, 'Social progress means the checking of the cosmic process at every step and the substitution for it of another which may be called the ethical process.'

He foresaw what he called ' . . . a constant struggle to maintain and improve, in opposition to the state of Nature, the state of Art of an organised polity; in which and by which men may develop a worthy civilisation capable of maintaining and constantly improving itself . . .' He did not foresee that this task, which he saw as a task for the human race, would in two generations be endangered not only by 'the cosmic process' but by stresses generated within what he called the ethical process itself. But if the prospect is even gloomier than it seemed to him, the issue is, I believe, exactly as he described it. The realization of form in human life, individual or collective, is, as he asserted, a work of artistry. It is an effort to impose on what he called the cosmic process a form which it would not take, if it were not conceived and imposed by men. But it is not only an individual but a collective work and it depends on a level of communication which is not yet in sight. This is through no fault of the communication engineers; we have facilities for communication far greater than we can use. The limitation, here as in all our problems, lies in the organization of senders and receivers which gives the communication meaning – in the setting of their appreciative systems. And it is this which – for good and ill – is becoming conscious of itself and drawn, inescapably, to take an ever firmer and more deliberate control of its own development.

This paper was originally given at a presentation at Brandeis University arranged jointly by the department of sociology and the Florence Heller Graduate School of Social Studies.

·9·

Science is Human

I. The Ubiquity of Psycho-social Science

The subject-matter of science includes men and their societies. The psycho-social sciences[1] are thus one among several branches of science; they accept the canons of science as worked out and followed by its elder branches and do their best to conform to those canons, as befits the more recently joined members of a club which has grown so much more exclusive since the days when the Royal Society was founded. The whole of science, on the other hand, is only one among many forms of human activity, all of which invite study by the psycho-social sciences; so even the most ancient and respected sciences are proper and necessary subject-matter for the youngest. In one respect they are the most proper and necessary of all; for science is widely regarded, not only by scientists, as the most characteristically human activity of man today, and the psycho-social sciences are especially concerned with what is characteristically human.

To explore the relations between two Chinese boxes, each of which claims to contain the other, is an intellectually intriguing adventure, calling for dialogue between the two viewpoints, which could not fail to be useful to both; but so far the psycho-

[1] In the psycho-social sciences I include all studies specially concerned with those aspects of men and their societies which are not shared with other species; notably social anthropology, sociology, part of psychology, the currently developing sciences of communication and control, and the sciences dealing with special aspects of human behaviour, notably economics, law, and political science. In the second section of the paper I define what I conceive to be the field common to these sciences. I use the expression 'social sciences' only when I intend it in its more customary sense.

social sciences have been diffident in exploring their elder siblings' activities – or even their own. Indeed, the mere suggestion that science is 'human' has vaguely affronting implications, likely to be followed by imputations of all those human failings from which science is supposed to guard us. These resistances themselves merit psycho-social study; for if we were asked to show what our species has achieved to warrant its pre-eminence, should we not parade our scientists? By the standards common to primates, a Rutherford, a Sherrington, a Freud are no small achievements. And how could we explain their emergence, except by reference to a socializing and humanizing process peculiar to our species, which had been operating for many millennia before the earliest science could be born and without which no potential astronomer could so much as notice a star? This process is central to the field of the psycho-social sciences.

We need not deplore – nor can we question – that science is a psycho-social activity.

The peculiar position of the psycho-social sciences may be described in a less provocative way. Like any other science, they have to place their subject-matter within the natural order, of which other aspects are explored by other sciences; and in doing so, they have to note the distinguishing characteristics which make it a convenient field for a separate science. (They should be able to tell us the likenesses and the differences between men and rats, between human societies and colonies of apes.) Further, within their chosen human field, they should be able to expound, at least better than the uninstructed, the likenesses and the differences between different human activities – of politicians, lawyers, and businessmen; likewise of preachers, criminals, and poets; and conspicuously of scientists, this last being an activity especially important, specific and familiar to them. Within this last field they should know the differences and relationships between the psycho-social sciences and the other sciences; in particular, any differences there may be between hypotheses made by men about men and their hypotheses about other matters. All these inquiries are important and interconnected; and all of them correspond with inquiries which any other science might be expected to answer about its subject-matter. But in the psycho-social sciences alone these questions and answers have a double impact. They bear ever more closely on the inquirer's own operations as well as on the objects of his attention, until they identify the two.

This is no doubt one reason why the psycho-social sciences have been on the whole as reluctant to explore their own activities as those of their fellow sciences.

The partial paralysis of the psycho-social sciences before the most interesting aspects of their subject-matter has a curious history. Before the rise of modern science, men supposed that they knew more about themselves and each other than about sticks, stones, and stars, which were more alien and less communicative; and they had no doubt that knowledge about men was more important than any other knowledge. Hence the former predominance of the humanities. Today, though their knowledge of themselves and each other is much greater, they value it less and mistrust it more. Indeed, they are uncertain how much of it to accept as knowledge at all. For physical science has been so successful that its methods have come to be regarded as the only acceptable road to knowledge and its criteria as the only acceptable measure of truth. Yet some of our most basic assumptions about ourselves and each other are neither derived by the methods nor validated by the criteria of the physical sciences. Moreover, it has been the task of science to cut man down to a size which could be fitted into the natural order and it has been reluctant to expand its idea of the natural order so as to make room for men – even for scientists. Yet this is clearly needed to accommodate those human phenomena which are furthest removed from the achievements of other creatures.

Happily, there has emerged, also from within the physical sciences, a liberalizing concept of still uncharted scope. The development of theory and technique in the field of communication and control has already produced, even in machines, models of regulative behaviour more sophisticated than the model most commonly used by psychologists to explain regulation in men. As the psycho-social sciences absorb the theory generated by communication engineers (even if they do not go beyond it), they are bound to develop a model of mental function more refined than has been attempted since behaviourism imposed its astringent limitations on their thinking; and this cannot fail to make a difference to the way in which men generally and scientists in particular view those of their activities which they regard as 'mental'.[1] It is already legitimizing several concepts which, however familiar and inescapable, have not hitherto been readily accommodated within the frontiers of the natural order, as recognized by the physical sciences, and have thus been subject to a subtle but effective intellectual ostracism.

In this paper, using these concepts, I shall offer answers to those questions posed earlier about the subject-matter of the psycho-social sciences, its relation to the subject-matter of other sciences, and its own sub-divisions, notably the sub-division which studies the human activity called science; a field of inquiry commonly called the philosophy of science, though it might, I think, be more specifically called scientific epistemology.

II. The Three Domains of Science

The first impact of this liberation is to clarify the field of the psycho-social sciences and its relation to the other sciences. It has long been apparent that the physical, the biological, and the psycho-social sciences are basically distinguished by their concentration on three distinct means of mediating change and continuity in the phenomena which they study. These have developed

---

[1] I use the word 'mental' throughout the paper to include all those processes which I describe later as appreciation. I believe that these processes are carried out by the brain and the central nervous system. We none the less need a word for them – and we should still need a word for them, even if we could specify the working of that organ in the minutest particular.

at different epochs in the history of our planet and are distinguished in common speech and common thought; but until
recently science has been reluctant to accept all the peculiarities
of the third or even of the second, because they could not easily
be accommodated within what the physical sciences sanctioned
as the bounds of the natural order. This restriction has now lost
its validity, though it will doubtless continue to haunt us for
some time.

Until the emergence of organic forms, change and continuity
were mediated only by transfers and transformations of energy.
The flow of winds along pressure gradients was explicable in
terms of the sun's heat, the earth's motion, and similar variables.
Evaporation and precipitation kept the water cycle turning,
regulated its distribution between the seas, the atmosphere, the
soil, and the deep reservoirs and, incidentally, eroded the moun-
tains which rose on the earth's contracting crust. The physical
sciences have compiled an astonishing corpus of theory and technique concerning the transformations and interactions of matter
and energy, which at this stage were solely involved. I will refer
to phenomena which are mediated in this way alone as 'energetic'.

This picture was notably changed by the emergence of organic
forms which, though equally subject to mechanical pushes and
pulls, thermal and chemical change and so on, were also responsive
to 'information'. This made possible both the internal organization of multicellular organisms and the net of external relationships which associate them with each other and with the rest of
their milieu. I will comprehend this change as the emergence of
responsiveness. In mediating external relationships, this depended
on the developing ability to distinguish sensory stimuli and to respond to them as signs and cues – cues for action, linked with
readiness to respond in particular ways; and signs for recognition,
linked with readinesses to recognize larger configurations of
objects or events with which such stimuli were or became
associated. Ethology, experimental psychology, and the psychology of perception compose a substantial and well-organized

body of theory about the operation of sensory stimuli as cues and signs, even though neurophysiology has not yet got far in unravelling the mechanisms by which these readinesses are developed, preserved, and activated.

In the human species this responsiveness has become the basis for a further development so far-reaching that it needs to be distinguished as a third stage, because it introduces not only a new means of mediating change but even a new dimension in which change can be mediated. This new dimension is the conceptual system whereby humans represent, interpret, value, and increasingly create the world in which they effectively live. The new mediator is human communication, notably dialogue and the internal procedures which have developed with its use. The conceptual system thus developed is a psycho-social artifact, of which the conceptual world created by science, with its attendant procedures, is the most stable, coherent, and explicit example. But business, politics, and other human activities have their own partly autonomous systems; and in each individual from birth to death is to be found, in self-directing and self-limiting development, an individual system as unique as his genetic code but containing initially far more possibilities than can be realized. These developments, individual and social, know springs and forms of change which have no counterpart in the purely responsive organization of other creatures. I will label the new mediator of change 'appreciation'.

According to this view, change and stability on the planet are now mediated in three distinguishable and coexistent ways – by transfers and transformations of energy, which are universally applicable to material objects; by responsiveness, which operates additionally and in various degrees in all organic forms (and an increasing number of artifacts); and by appreciation, which operates as a third and further mediator among those organic (and other) forms which are or become capable of it. The independence of the three modes is as important as their interrelation. A densely packed crowd leaving a public square will distribute its volume between the different exits according to their capacity in a manner which, at first, would obey the laws governing the flow of water from a cistern. As soon as the pressure became less, individual units would begin to avoid physical collision in a way which could only be explained by crediting them with responsiveness. Later still, each individual would begin to go its own way in a manner which would only be explicable by reference to the current setting of what I shall describe as its appreciative system.

In a world in which organic forms proliferate and humans have become dominant, the second mode of mediating change grows in importance relatively to the first, and the third relatively to the first and second. The third and peculiarly human mode has a further interest for us, because we happen to be human. It is ironic – and may well become tragic – that its importance should be obscured by its originality.

The responsiveness of organisms has been a matter of common observation for millennia and has always provided the most common practical distinction between organic forms and inorganic matter. The biological and psycho-social sciences, however, were slow to chart the full distinction between energy transfer and responsiveness, because the physical sciences until recently appeared to leave no room for it.

> 'Even the word "motivation" has an archaic ring, reminiscent of the days when minds seeking an explanation for a happening were wont to seek first for a "mover" and ultimately for a "prime mover". "Drive", with which some writers seem to identify motivation, has even stronger energetic connotations' (pp. 135–6 above).

Minds still dwelt in a Newtonian world, where bodies remained at rest until something moved them and in which, therefore, the explanation for the direction, no less than the speed, of the movement was to be sought, at least in part, in the 'mover'.

In dynamic systems, however, stablity, not change, requires explanation. The regularities and stabilities of the atmosphere, still unresponsive to 'information', are exceptional in an increasingly organic world, where the direction and control of energy is increasingly separable, as a field of study, from its generation. Biologists have long distinguished refined controls within the organism operated by no more energy than is needed to transmit a signal. None the less, these signal-mediated changes remained for long anomalous, as not clearly to be reconciled with a mechanistic world; still less so were the subtler secrets of the genetic code. And indeed, they were not to be reconciled with the mechanistic world of the nineteenth century. Driesch, lacking today's answer, had no alternative but to posit an unknown (by whatever name he called it) to account for the ability of his mutilated embryos to complete themselves; or, for that matter, for the more obvious ability of living tissue to repair damage.

The mechanist-vitalist controversy haunted science – usefully, since it kept alive a critical, unanswered question – until physicists, grappling with the practical problems of telecommunication, defined the concept of information theoretically and explained signal-mediated changes as choices made in response to information by a selector, according to rules built into or developed by the selector, between alternatives, none of which was excluded for lack of energy. This formulation, even in its simplest form, was a gift both for biology and for psychology. The old S–R psychology implicitly assumed its organisms to be by nature as much at rest as unmoved objects in Newtonian space, needing 'stimulus' to move them to anything at all. The later ethological concept of the cue as a 'releaser'[1] rather than a stimulus was a welcome corrective; but it was devised for innate mechanisms where the response was built in, the only question being whether the combination of the cue with the state of the organism is sufficient to release the response.[2] Communication engineers offered a concept and a model which could explain a much wider

[1] An expression first coined, I believe, by N. Tinbergen in *The Study of Instinct* (1951).

[2] Though 'displacement activities' constitute an exception of some significance (Tinbergen, N., 1951, p. 113).

variety of outcomes in terms of the impact of information on a selector. The energy to effect the outcome could simply be taken for granted.

So today a biochemist studying an enzyme system as a regulator of growth moves without embarrassment in a universe of discourse different from that of his fellow biochemist studying the same enzyme system as a link in the process of energy transformation; just as an engineer devising and programming the control system of a rocket uses concepts remote from those of his colleague concerned with its propulsion.

Before this liberation, animal experimenters and learning theorists had not advanced confidently beyond the model of the hungry rat – the goal-seeking, problem-solving creature whose goal was given and whose sole problem at any time was to devise or remember an appropriate response. The readiness to respond lay latent from one occasion to another, reinforced by repeated, successful use, weakened and in time extinguished by disuse or non-success. The criteria of success were supposed to be built in. This model permeated our culture long before biological science gave it scientific precision. The economic man was a hungry rat.

The concepts and theories of information, communication, and control provide even today a model of regulation more refined than the hungry rat. They do not of themselves tell us anything certain about the ways in which the human brain and CNS receive, store, and process information. Still less do they tell us about the means whereby these capacities are organized in a particular way to give particular meaning to information which they may receive or generate. They do not even require us to assume that the brain and CNS work in a manner analogous to any combination of analogue and digital computers which engineers can model. They do, however, provide a scientifically respectable set of ideas capable of comprehending *more than* the degree of responsiveness which men share with other creatures. They thus shift the frontier of uncertainty and open the way to the scientific understanding of some at least of those realities of common experience which I am subsuming under the concept of appreciation.

How far along that road they will take us is, as I shall seek to show later, still uncertain.

III. The Phenomena of 'Appreciation'

These new concepts serve to make acceptable some of the more puzzling features of appreciation which are already known. For despite the difficulty of using an instrument (the appreciative system) to explore itself, the psycho-social sciences have already compiled an important body of knowledge about it. This has been gathered chiefly in the fields of child development (where it can be watched in growth); of cultural anthropology (where it can be watched in a culture other than the observer's); and of psychiatry (where it can be watched in pathological disturbance). I will mention those established conclusions which are most to my purpose.

Irrespective of culture, all children (including the greatest future scientists) start life unable to distinguish one thing from another or even self from non-self; equipped, so far as we know, only with a few reflexes, an unique genetic code, and a learning potential.[1] They are socialized and humanized by being talked to and encouraged to respond to talk at at a critical, early age. The classic case in which the power of human communication to socialize and humanize triumphed without the help of either hearing or sight has thrown much light on the process.[2]

This circular process of 'education' is seen at its simplest and best attested in the growth of perception. The child must learn even to 'see'. Perfect vision conveys no message to the mind, until experience has built up schemata to order the 'blooming, buzzing

[1] Though Susanne Langer (1957) has postulated in humans a 'need to symbolize' which, if it exists, should perhaps not be dismissed as one of 'a few reflexes'.
[2] See Helen Keller (1920), especially the often quoted passage in which she recalls the moment when she suddenly appreciated the significance of names in classifying experience.

confusion'. Adult students learning to read a pulmonary radio-graph are in like case; only the repeated scanning of examples builds up the schema with which to recognize future examples. The emergent schemata are both the product and the mediator of the change. The process is most dramatically illustrated by the distressful time of conscious learning experienced by those born blind who acquire sight first in adult life.[1]

These schemata are 'readinesses to see' things in one way, rather than another; habits of selecting and grouping for attention, which develop cognition out of recognition. Facilitating the seeing of things one way, they impede the subsequent seeing of them in any other way. It is as hard for the teacher to ignore the schema which makes a pulmonary radiograph significant as it is for his student to learn it.

Not only perception but all cognition depends on recognition by the use of schemata. The lawyer learns to distinguish situations giving rise to legal liability from those which do not; to distinguish those that create only civil liability from those which also constitute crimes; to distinguish civil liability deriving from contract from that which is based on 'tort'. His mental processes appear to be the same as those of the doctor learning to diagnose diseases, although, unlike the doctor, he relies not at all on visually manifest cues. Whatever the mind can represent to itself, from a cow to a contract, from a law of nature to a legal principle, is recognized by applying schemata – 'readinesses to see' which are themselves developed or restricted, confirmed or confused, ela-borated or simplified, by their further use. The unfamiliar is liable to be subsumed under schemata which are seen later to be grossly inadequate or inept. Anything so unfamiliar that no existing schema can be bent or stretched to contain it passes in blank in-comprehension – until further experience evokes an ordering schema.

This circular process, which contains the real answer to all conundrums of the 'hen-and-egg' type, is ubiquitous through the

[1] The evidence is conveniently summarized in Abercrombie (1960).

whole range of human learning. It is the commonest fact of life – and the first foundation for a scientific epistemology. It is conceptually baffling only because our ideas of how change is mediated are still limited by scientific concepts inadequate to the phenomena of appreciation or even of responsiveness.

Language may not be the only factor which develops this organizing faculty in the human brain to a degree so far beyond that of other creatures; but comparative studies of children and young primates show that it is crucial, and this need not surprise us. Language provides a new channel of immense capacity for expanding 'input' and eliciting 'output'. It provides a symbolism whereby anything within the individual's repertory can be activated, whether any of the 'facts' symbolized are present or possible or not; and this in turn provides a basis for procedures whereby further 'input' can be internally generated. It seems clearly to play the key role in calling into being the new dimension in which humans develop the forms we know as personalities, cultures, and institutions.[1]

An outstanding characteristic of the circular process is its capacity for admitting change without losing continuity. The child is at first an uncritical recipient of the information with which it is flooded; for the schemata for criticism must themselves be generated by the same process. It is therefore strange beyond measure that each generation, in the course of taking over its heritage, rejects, adds, and changes so much. (Only ten generations separate us from Newton; only thirty from Alfred the Great.) This rate of change is the stranger when we reflect that the schemata by which our conceptual world is organized are mutually related, organized in a system of which no part can be changed without widespread disturbance and which must remain reasonably coherent, if it is to serve effectively as an interpreter of experience, a basis for communication, and a guide to action.

[1] The significance of other symbolic systems, mathematical, musical, graphical, and so on will not be considered here, because they seem to me peripheral to the argument; not because I think them unimportant.

The circular process observed in child development and adult learning is equally ubiquitous at the level studied by sociologists and social anthropologists and its 'self-determining' aspect is no less marked. It is as well exemplified by the growth of the law as by the learning process of the lawyer. The law consists essentially in schemata by which aspects of transactions are distinguished and evaluated; but it is only in recent times, under the influence of sociology, that jurists have accepted the view that these schemata are generated and changed by the very process of applying them.[1] The circularity of the process appears conspicuously in the use made by British and American law of deliberately open concepts such as the 'reasonable man'. What care would a reasonable man take of his own property? In what circumstances would a reasonable man feel justified in defending himself with force? The answers are crucial for some purposes but the law does not answer them in general terms. It will only point to concrete examples in the past in which such actions have been held to be reasonable or the reverse. Each new decision adds to and changes the underlying schema; so the reasonable man remains perpetually young, changing his standards with the passage of time and quietly contributing to the changes which he is supposed to reflect.

The Barotse, a people of Northern Rhodesia, had, at least until recently, an undeveloped economy; but they had a well-developed system of law which contrasts sometimes sharply – and not always unfavourably – with that of their British ex-administrators, yet parallels it closely in most fundamentals. It makes even more extensive use of the reasonable man – a reasonable Barotse man, whose expected responses, often familiar to a Briton, awaken sometimes surprise and occasionally admiration or envy. It aspires sometimes to do more comprehensive 'justice' than British courts attempt,[2] but its conception of justice is wholly familiar. A

[1] For a recent exposition of this theme see Friedmann (1959).

[2] Significantly, only children's courts in our culture still treat the particular contravention of the law which engages their attention (as the Barotse do) primarily as a symptom of some deeper disorder of the system which should be their real concern.

British or American lawyer, reading Professor Gluckman's fascinating account (1955) of the judicial process among the Barotse, will see not only their system but his own also as an 'appreciative system', forming part of a culture and constantly in development by a circular process of which it is both the chief product and the chief architect.

Too often studies of this kind compare some state of affairs which is deemed 'abnormal', even pathological, with an accepted norm which is not further explored. Studies of race prejudice sometimes take this form, and for some purposes it is legitimate; but it conceals the fact that every norm, however well accepted, is itself an artifact and itself in process of change. Race prejudice often has psychopathological features; yet its absence is itself a cultural norm no less artifactual than its opposite – more so, indeed, for the ability to ignore conspicuous perceptual differences in favour of less obvious but more significant similarities is a sophisticated development of the appreciative system.

The powers which are thus visible in child development and in cross-cultural studies are clearly the main distinguishing features of humankind and must presumably be seated in uniquely developed capacities of the human brain and CNS. Yet psychology, in so far as it has studied the internal constituents of the human personality, has not yet deeply explored them. The volume of work done on 'thinking', important as it is, seems strangely small, having regard to the fact that departments of psychology are found in communities where thinking is so conspicuous an activity. This is doubtless due in part to lack of suitable research methods; partly to preoccupations with the more amenable characteristics which men share with other creatures; partly, perhaps, to fear of the complexities which must follow the admission, as a subject for study, of an appreciative system enjoying even a partial autonomy to generate its own criteria; partly to the unscientific connotation which has become attached to the idea that men, even scientists, have 'minds' as well as 'brains'.[1]

[1] See footnote on p. 176.

'Dynamic' psychology provides an exception of only limited relevance, because of its concentration on unconscious processes in pathological disarray. To concentrate on minds which are conceived as estranged from 'reality', necessary and legitimate as it is in psychiatry, is bound to obscure the fact that, even for the sane, reality is no less an artifact than a fact. 'The sanest, like the maddest of us cling like spiders to a self-spun web, obscurely moored in vacancy and fiercely shaken by the winds of change' (Vickers, 1964).

IV. A Formulation of 'Appreciation'

Clearly, we must credit ourselves with a socially developed capacity for interpreting experience, a capacity on which scientists, no less than other men, rely absolutely, yet which is within their capacity to develop, criticize, and change. It is curious that this capacity has no generally accepted name. I am therefore obliged to coin some terms to describe it. I do so reluctantly, insisting that I am not inventing new abstractions but simply naming well-established capacities of our kind. For it is, I think, undeniable, especially among scientists, that men develop, largely through communication and the mental activities which it engenders, an enduring yet changing conceptual world, partly though never wholly shared by the members of the communicating group and that this great psycho-social artifact subsists in patterns of organization in individual brains.

I will describe this system of schemata by means of which our world is ordered as a 'reality system', although it is capable of representing the hypothetical, as well as the actual. But even the examples given show that it has another constituent. What selects these, rather than other aspects of reality for our attention? What kinds of attention are bestowed on them? They are selected because they are relevant to the needs of the creatures that select them, and the kinds of attention bestowed on them are as various as the needs; but these 'needs' have become immensely varied by the same process as has generated so complex a reality system. Creators of a multiple, enduring, inner world, men have become free to develop multiple, enduring interests – for example, the interests of all the sciences. Possessed by multiple interests, they develop multiple expectations; and these generate multiple aspirations, constituting standards by which to judge what is and what might be. Our world of reality is selected and structured by our interests and by the standards which our interests generate. I will comprehend these in the term 'value' (without implying that they exhaust it). The development of these interests and standards is as apparent in child development, in the growth of institutions, and in cultural change as is the growth of the corresponding reality system. They too are 'readinesses', readinesses to value, related to readinesses to see. They too are systematically organized, a value system, distinguishable from the reality system yet inseparable from it. For facts are relevant only by reference to some judgement of value and judgements of value are meaningful only in regard to some configuration of fact. Hence the need for a word to embrace the two, for which I propose 'appreciation', a word, not yet appropriated by science, which in its ordinary use (as in 'appreciation of a situation') implies a combined judgement of value and fact.

I use the terms 'reality system' and 'value system' to describe the two complementary aspects of this organization, and 'appreciative system' to describe them in the association in which they are always found. I describe the actual state of such a system at any time as its setting and any exercise of it as a judgement. And I would stress that the actual setting of such a system can never be known, since it is manifest only in a judgement, the making of which may have changed the setting of the system – a fact experienced not only by litigants in leading cases but by everyone who has taken part in the always fascinating, sometimes agonizing, and often surprising exercise of making up an individual or a collective mind.[1]

[1] I have developed these ideas at greater length in *The Art of Judgment* (1965).

It is unsatisfactory to posit processes, the working of which cannot be modelled; but science must often do so. It hesitates only when the assumption to be made is suspect – that is, when it invites classification by some schema to which an adverse scientific value is attached. So it is welcome that these speculations about mental process should take a form so similar to that which communication engineers have now legitimized. Everyone has now become familiar with the elements of automatic control. An automatic pilot, for example, must know how the ship's head is swinging and it must know the course. Only by comparing the two – comparing 'what is' with 'what ought to be' – can it derive a signal to select an appropriate rudder movement. It cannot make the 'appreciation' which leads to selective action, unless it has both the relevant information and the standard which gives the information meaning *for it*.[1] It would be absurd to suppose that the human mind, which, whatever else it does, clearly functions as a regulator, would or could select facts without values to make them relevant. The illusion that science does just this has contributed much to obscuring the real problems associated with value.

This analogy with control mechanisms defines *three* dimensions in which learning is theoretically possible; for the simplest control mechanism has three capacities – to receive information, to compare it with a standard, and, in response to the comparison, to select a response, be this only to make or withhold the only response of which it is capable. In highly developed systems all three capacities become extensible by learning. Our complacency as a species usually derives from our superiority in the first and third. We are wonderful at collecting, classifying, and storing information and processing it to produce more information and novel classification – our developing reality system. We have already far more information than we can use. We are wonderful, also, at selecting action – not merely at choosing from an ever wider

[1] 'The information given by a compass . . . when fed to an automatic pilot, has a meaning different from what it would have, if fed to a device for keeping a running record of position by dead reckoning' (Vickers, 1965, p. 40).

repertory but at enlarging the repertory and so developing an expanding system of readinesses for action.

We are much less impressed by our learning achievements, individual or collective, in the dimension of value; and indeed they are much less impressive. Yet the most cursory glance at the history of an individual, a society, or a nation discloses learning, unlearning, and relearning in the field of values, changes in the focus of interest and in the evaluating standard, at least as great and as important as the corresponding changes in the realms of information and action.

'Men, institutions and societies learn what to want as well as how to get, what to be as well as what to do; and the two forms of adaptation are closely related. Since our ideas of regulation were formed in relation to norms which are deemed to be given, they need to be reconsidered in relation to norms which change with the effort made to pursue them' (Vickers, 1964).

The more successful human examples, individual and collective, show the growth of a value system both more complex and better integrated, capable of guiding the pursuit of disparate and often conflicting values. Some may even think that it shows some accumulation of tested knowledge. The capacity for developing their value systems distinguishes men from other creatures far more sharply than their enhanced capacities for cognition and action and poses far more important problems of learning and of teaching.

Viewing the bewildering variety and changeability of the interests and standards which govern human behaviour, scientists have made ingenious efforts to simplify them. They need not, as I suggest, be reduced to a pattern simpler than the ones which communication engineers already build into control mechanisms; and they cannot as yet be reduced even to that pattern. An automatic factory has to maintain itself as a going concern, regulating to this end both the internal relations which enable it to act as a whole and the external ones by which it maintains supportive relations with its milieu. But not any set of

193

self-maintaining relations will do. The factory has to maintain a production programme and may find its problem-solving capacity strained to the utmost by the programme which it is given. Men and institutions are in like case; they have not only to survive but to function. They differ from present automata only in the important particular that they are constantly required, both by the demands of the milieu and by their own settings, to maintain disparate and mutually limiting relations and hence to make multi-valued choices. Every government settling its budget has to decide – or discover – what combination of mutually limiting objectives it should pursue and has no means to derive one right answer from its premises; and the same is true of every individual. The regulative function is thus a double one – to maintain the dynamic balance of the system and to 'optimize' the relations to be realized or maintained. Both parts of the function, balancing and optimizing, are developed by learning – learning not merely how to maintain a given set of relations but what set to regard as optimal.[1]

The theories and models of communication engineers do not yet give us much guidance on the ways in which value systems develop and conflicts of value are resolved; but they enable us to state the problem as one to be expected among creatures such as we now conceive ourselves to be. They relieve any anxiety we might have had at admitting 'readinesses' as objects of our attention. They make it clear that information conveys no meaning to a regulator, human or automatic, unless that regulator has some standard of evaluation. And they lead us to expect that such standards will be generated by the circular process I have described and will pose, as they develop, exactly the problems of conflicting values, whether in the same or in different minds, which so conspicuously plague us and which have so often been regarded as a scientific indecency.

[1] This idea is more fully developed in *The Art of Judgment* (1965).

V. Science as a Psycho-social Activity

The brain is clearly the main organ for regulating relations between creatures which have developed one and their milieu. I have suggested that the main difference between man and other 'brainy' creatures, as they appear from the findings of the sciences which study him, is the development of this regulator in *all three* of the dimensions in which a regulator can develop. If we look at any individual, we shall see reality system, value system, and action system developing through life in close interconnection, whatever his occupation. But if we look at the society of which he forms part, we may regard the scientists as the main (official) architects of the reality system and the technologists as the main (official) architects of its action system, while the politicians are probably the most conspicuous architects of its value system.

The crudity of this classification will serve to remind us how much knowledge we possess which no one would credit to science; how much of our manipulations of the milieu escapes classification as technology; and how unidentified are most of the sources from which we learn our values. None the less, the classification will serve as a starting-point from which to explore the peculiarities of science as a human activity; for these derive from the constancy and simplicity of its values – of what it is trying to do. It is trying to develop the reality system *for its own sake*. Politicians, technologists, and businessmen are concerned with what to seek and how to seek it; their interest in the way things are is generated and directed by their interest in how it might be. The scientist's interest is in understanding how it is.

It is convenient, though dangerous, to refer to a reality system – or any current setting of it – as a map and to the scientist as a map-maker. The analogy is dangerous, partly because our reality systems represent temporal and causal, as well as spatial relations; partly because they map the hypothetical as well as the actual and thus produce plans as well as maps; partly because some of the facts which they represent are themselves features of the appreciative system. More fundamentally, it is dangerous because we conceive a map as having a one-to-one relationship with the features which it represents; and this is precisely the kind of knowledge which sub-atomic scientists (unlike Newton) commonly disclaim. None the less, I shall use the simile, because it is valid enough over large areas of experience, as a means of exploring the values of science.

A map is and must be highly selective. It cannot include 'everything'; and even 'everything' would be only 'everything which that map-maker's repertory of schemata could distinguish'. In fact, most maps are much more selective; motoring-maps, walking-maps, geological maps, military maps distinguish different sets of features, selected by the interest which dominates the map-maker's mind at the time.

The map-maker has his own interest, as a map-maker, in relating the selected features of a particular bit of physical environment to one another; an example of that urge to 'make sense' of our milieu which is one of the most universal of human interests and at the same time the one most characteristic of science. As a map-maker, he has also a set of standards (not wholly consistent) – standards of accuracy, of comprehensiveness, of consistency, of relevance, of legibility, and of elegance – which apply to all maps and by which alone he can value his achievement as a map-maker. As a map-maker, he is not interested in whether the facts he represents are as map-*users* might wish them to be for the purpose of their diverse interests, nor would they wish him to be; for this ensures his freedom from bias by those interests proper to men other than map-makers and thus his usefulness to them. It also fosters the absurd legend that he is not concerned with 'values'.

He is, of course, as much concerned with and moved by values as anyone else; but *as a map-maker* he is concerned only with the values appropriate to map-making. Being also human and thus more and less than the embodiment of a single role, his value

196

system is of course far more complicated and has far more in common with his fellows' than this analysis allows; but I am considering him solely in his capacity as a scientist.

There is something definable and hence to our age peculiarly precious about the values of the scientist. Varied though his interests are, he is deemed to be moved by one paramount value, once called truth but now more modestly referred to as reliability in the maps he makes. Further, and much more unusually, he has means to confirm or disprove his accuracy which are accepted by and accessible to all his fellows and he claims to be not interested in 'facts' which cannot be so disproved or progressively confirmed. In almost all their other activities, institutional and personal, men (like governments in an earlier example) pursue disparate and conflicting interests, apply disparate and conflicting standards, and reconcile their conflicts by acts of judgement which can never be proved correct or incorrect but only endorsed as good or condemned as bad by like judgements of other minds. The making of these multi-valued choices is the aspect of human behaviour which is hardest to corral within the natural order as formerly understood, and it was correspondingly satisfying to believe that the pursuit of scientific truth was free from this obscurity. For in science alone (so the myth runs) success is measured by only one criterion, to which all can appeal, by which all are bound, and which none can alter. That (says the myth) is why the achievements of science are cumulative, while those of politics, ethics, and art are not.

The myth enshrines an important truth, over-simplified and exaggerated though it be. Although science has two tests of truth which often conflict and other standards also, it remains true that the values of map-makers are simpler, less conflicting, more amenable to test, and more widely held in common than are the multiple and conflicting values of all the diverse map-*users*. Journeys are infinitely varied and fashions may change, in journeys as in other things; but maps are affected by such changes only in so far as their makers are thereby led to omit some features and emphasize others.

Thus the word 'scientific' carries a reassuring overtone of constancy and certainty, which reflects the limitations of its own objectives.

We use the word scientific not only to define the set of values peculiar to science, the map-maker's values, but also to define a method which has proved hugely productive in the making of serviceable maps and a kind and degree of assurance which the method can yield. In all three contexts its meaning differs significantly from one branch of science to another. So anything which can be said of science in general has to be said in very general terms.

The basic attitude of science, as I understand it, is to treat all our beliefs as more or less established hypotheses, commitment to which, though necessary, is hazardous,[1] since, as features of our appreciative system, they are bound to grow and change. They should therefore be continually tested and accorded credence related to the results of these tests. The criteria for testing are two-fold and often conflict; they are the ancient tests of 'correspondence' and 'coherence' (though 'correspondence' has a more modest significance nowadays than it once had). In testing for correspondence we ask first whether the hypothesis explains the course of events which evoked it; then, whether it is consistent with other known courses of event; and further, where this is possible, whether predictions based on it are confirmed by event. (In each case, 'event' – at least in the physical sciences – means the result of some observational procedure.) In testing for coherence, we ask whether the hypothesis can be admitted to our reality system without unacceptable disturbance of other hypotheses; and further, whether its admission will clear up other areas of confusion beside the one which evoked it. Every accepted hypothesis, in its heyday, passes both tests with convincing, if not complete, success; but nearly every important hypothesis, at its inception, creates difficulties in one field or the other and must both wait

[1] Professor Michael Polanyi has developed the idea of scientific theories as 'hazardous commitments' in *Personal Knowledge* (1958).

and fight for admission. The history of science is littered with such controversies.[1]

This view of scientific method assumes that all scientific activity starts with a problem.[2] By a problem I understand the felt need to remove some disparity thrown up by the appreciative system. The disparity may be between the actual results of some experiment and the results which are to be expected according to current theory – like the results of the Michelson-Morley experiments. It may be a disparity between two features of the appreciative system itself – like the need to reconcile the concepts of 'wave' and 'particle'. The most radical problems often arise from recognizing as unexplained some feature of the appreciative system which has lain too deeply accepted for examination – as when Einstein first questioned the conventional concept of time.[3] Sometimes the problem is to amplify the system in some respect in which it appears to be incomplete or inconvenient or merely inelegant.

Each tentative solution is an hypothesis to which credence attaches progressively, both through the accumulation of instances in which it holds and through the development of further hypotheses dependent on the first and thus supportive of it. These

[1] For a dramatic and well-documented example, see the paper by Polanyi (1963), 'The Potential Theory of Adsorption'. This theory, first advanced by the author in 1914, was received favourably at first; then rejected because other theories in other contexts made it appear that cohesive forces should be explained by electrical interactions; reinstated ten years later, when a new theory of cohesive forces made it again acceptable; but accepted in fact only after a further passage of time. Throughout the decades of its eclipse, its experimental validation remained unchallenged. Professor Polanyi concludes that this 'mis-carriage of the scientific method' was unavoidable. None the less, 'Professionally, I survived . . . only by the skin of my teeth.' Scientific orthodoxy is enforced today, at least in Western countries, by a discipline more rigorous than any other orthodoxy.

[2] A position strongly argued by Professor Karl Popper in *The Poverty of Historicism* (1957).

[3] 'It was then [as a pupil in the Gymnasium] that the great problem really started to trouble him [Einstein]. He was intensely concerned with it for seven years; from the moment, however, that he came to question the customary concept of time . . . it took him only five weeks to write his paper on relativity – although at this time he was doing a full day's work at the Patent Office' (Wertheimer, 1959, p. 214).

procedures yield degrees of assurance ranging from near-certainty to remote possibility. Complete certainty is not attainable[1] but disproof is usually possible. An hypothesis incapable of disproof is usually regarded as outside the realm of science. Some would refuse to dignify by the name of theory any hypothesis which had not been validated by prediction.

These procedures do not differ in principle from those by which men have always developed their understanding of the world they live in. Long before 'science' existed, men formed expectations based on experience and revised them in the light of further experience. Science performed a double task – positively, to formulate and develop this procedure in all its rigour and ingenuity; negatively, to challenge, not all authority, but all authority except its own.

These problem-solving activities can be modelled, at least to some extent, by communication engineers and their models have thrown light on problem-solving by men, including scientists. The area least modelled and least understood is the way in which hypotheses are generated.

VI. Peculiarities of the Psycho-social Sciences

The methods of science were worked out in the study of 'energetic' phenomena, the constituents of which, since they do not learn, are amenable to repeated observation and experiment in conditions known to be constant or differing only in known ways. They grow less informative as the phenomena to which they are directed become more dependent on responsiveness and apprecia-

[1] I omit reference to those epistemological sources of validation, which, as Eddington observed, prove completely, if at all. To compress his luminous illustration – an ichthyologist, sampling the ocean with a given net might conclude experimentally (1) that no sea creature is less than two inches long and (2) that all sea creatures have gills. Experiment could only yield progressive confirmation of the first and ultimate disproof of the second. But a knowledge of the net would show that the first was necessarily true if the subject-matter were defined as 'catchable fish' and necessarily unprovable if it were not. He persuasively argues the case for confining physics, though not necessarily other sciences, to the study of 'catchable fish' (Eddington, 1949, esp. pp. 68, 69).

tion. Behaviour dependent on human communication is the least congenial to the methods of the physical sciences; for it depends on the appreciative settings of the participants, which alone give meaning to the communications they receive. This setting cannot be observed; it can only be inferred after the event and it changes with the events which reveal it. To take a very simple example – the meaning for me of a communication which I am about to receive will depend in part on whether I believe it; but my belief in it will depend in part on the impact which it makes on me when I hear it. So the appreciative system with which I await it may be radically reset by the activity of responding to it. Thus the setting of the appreciative system, personal and collective, is more uniquely self-determined by the cyclical process already noticed and thus more 'historical' than any other phenomenon which we need to understand.

A sharp distinction is often drawn between historical and scientific explanation. Since phenomena in the psycho-social field are so incurably historical, it is useful to consider the relation between the two types of explanation.

To be fully explicable in scientific terms, an event must at present be (as Warren Weaver (1948) put it) either of such 'organized simplicity' that it can be expressed in terms of invariant laws and limiting conditions or of such 'unorganized complexity' that it can be handled statistically. Many events elude both these categories; they are of such 'organized complexity' that they can at present be described only historically. This may be, as I have suggested, because in the field mediated by appreciation the conditions on which any regularity depends are constantly being changed by the very activity which expresses them; or it may be because the laws and limiting conditions involved, though all known in principle, are too complex and too unascertainable to be useful.

In one or both of these senses an avalanche, an epidemic, and a riot are all historical events. Though some things can be said in general about avalanches, epidemics, and riots, any individual of the class is uniquely determined. Scientifically, we know more about the laws and limiting conditions governing avalanches (a purely 'energetic' phenomenon) than about those governing epidemics (which also involve responsiveness); more about epidemics than about riots (which also involve appreciation). Indeed, I suppose that physicists can state completely the laws and limiting conditions which determine whether snow will lie on a slope and when, after it starts to slip, it will come to rest. But the conditions of any particular slope are so complex and so impossible to ascertain without disturbing them that those concerned to assess its safety must still largely rely on visual cues and general experience of the conditions in which avalanches are likely to occur.

The laws which define vulnerability and resistance to disease and the conditions in which interacting vulnerabilities will snowball into an epidemic are far less precisely known; and even more speculative are the psychological laws which keep citizens compliant with the laws of the land. Yet even if all these were far better known, they would not necessarily increase the power to *predict* the occurrence of an epidemic or a riot. None the less, what we know about the relevant laws and conditions in all three cases is extremely useful both before and after the event. Apart from assuring us that the event is not the expression of sorcery or divine vengeance – no small revision in the once accepted setting of our appreciative systems – it enables us to describe the main conditions making for stability and instability in the relevant fields and thus to guide policy both before and after the event. The second is no less important than the first; the value which the physical sciences have taught us to attach to prediction leads us to underrate the value of hindsight, especially in the psycho-social field. It will be as important, after the event, to understand why the riot occurred, as it was, earlier, to understand its imminence.

The example will serve to illustrate the difficulties of prediction in the psycho-social field. Suppose that in anticipation of the riot, the authorities arrested the suspected ringleader. It is reasonably certain that this will prevent him from doing any of the things which he could have done if he had been physically free; but its main effect is almost certainly as a communication indicative of the authority's attitudes and intentions. As such, it affects in diverse ways both the expectations which people have of the authority and their attitudes towards it. Neither is predictable. Some will read the communication as evidence of weakness, others of strength. In some it will evoke fear, in others resentment, in some assurance, in others anxiety. It will both strengthen and weaken the will to rebel. Its overall effect depends on the settings of innumerable appreciative systems.

Meantime, the act has changed the external situation in a way which time will further change; for the arrested man must either be detained for a period which will grow more significant as it lengthens or be released, an act which will not restore the *status quo*, because it will have its own significance as a further communication.

Hence, although authorities have been dealing with riots and impending riots since the first ruler commanded power, the only relevant principles which can be regarded as validated by anything approaching scientific method are those in the fields of 'energetics' and, to a less degree, of responsiveness. What barriers will restrain what weight of surging crowd is largely a problem of energetics. What deployment of dogs, tear gas, and fire hoses will disperse what crowd is largely a problem of responsiveness. On both these, I imagine that the police forces of the world possess a fund of tested knowledge, reliable in the first case, useful in the second. But what kind of communication will provoke, avert, or still a riot depends on the manifold appreciative settings of all the people concerned, a variable with a range of variety greater by many orders of magnitude. In a field of such vast and unverified variety dogmas can subsist for millennia, incapable alike of proof and disproof or – worse – potent to ensure their own validation.

It is, of course, possible to carve out from the subject-matter of the social sciences regularities which can be studied by the methods of the other sciences, notably by statistical method. But it is important, I suggest, not to confine psycho-social inquiry to the sometimes trivial topics which can be so isolated; still more to avoid dressing up psycho-social inquiries in pseudo-scientific clothes. For the fact is that we possess and rely on a fund of knowledge about men and societies far greater than we should expect to possess, if we had no other source of knowledge than we have in the other domains of science; and we shall do well to inquire more closely than is usually done into the sources of assurance on which we are accustomed to act. For the relation of the scientist to his subject-matter in the psycho-social sciences differs in important ways from that relation in the other sciences. The hypotheses which he forms are both generated and validated in ways which are significantly different.

One of these differences seems clear to me, though it is seldom admitted, except in a limited field of psychiatry. We know what it is to be human in a way in which we know nothing else; and we cannot help attributing to those whom we regard as human private experiences similar to our own, although the two can be compared only by the obscure means of dialogue. These assumptions we withdraw only if 'experience' disproves them – experience including the experience of dialogue. In the meantime, an unconscious web of assumptions structures and fills in our knowledge of our fellow-men, often right, sometimes grotesquely wrong, never more than fractionally verified or even identified, yet indispensable as a base to the fabric of expectation on which our appreciative system stands.

If this is right, we must accept as a fact, perhaps scientifically unfortunate but inescapable and on balance undoubtedly useful, that every psycho-social scientist starts work with a whole system of assumptions about his subject-matter, derived from a source which is not relevant to other sciences, which is largely unverifiable by what we accept formally as the conventional methods of science; which is often unconscious, sometimes even undisprovable; and which yet yields a high degree of assurance.

The full implications of this – for good and ill – have not yet been charted. It is time they were; for if it be agreed that science is able to exist only because scientists can talk to each other, it cannot be immaterial or wholly to the bad that some of them can talk with their subject-matter also.

A further difference, though more familiar, is no less radical. Human communication is potent to change the appreciative systems of all who share in the communication. In the physical sciences the objects of attention do not participate in the scientists' discussions and are unchanged by their activities, except at the sub-atomic level. In the psycho-social sciences the reverse is true. Only the limiting case approximates to what in the physical sciences is normal. The anthropologist, participating in the life of a primitive tribe, may leave the object of his attention only slightly disturbed by his presence and by his subsequent publications; but where he studies his own culture, these supposedly optimal conditions break down. Indeed, they are usually *intended* to break down. Hence the inescapably polemical nature of all social surveys. Once the social scientist has said – 'This is how it is', the subject-matter of his descriptions can never be the same again; for the relations that made it and kept it so have been irreversibly changed, merely by being brought to the level of conscious attention.

It remains to mention what is perhaps the most important distinction between the subject-matter of the psycho-social and the physical sciences. The regularities observable among men are predominantly those evolved by their own societies. These depend on a tissue of mutual expectations, which members of a society are by and large set to preserve. The reason why the future behaviour of fellow-men is in fact so much more predictable than the weather, although we know so much less about the variables which control it, is that they are concerned to *be* predictable; to fulfil the expectations of their neighbours and to act in the faith that their neighbours will do the same by them. The regularities of human behaviour, which at their most human are far more resistant to disturbance than those of systems mediated only by energy flow and responsiveness, are themselves an artifact, the product of the regulator which is the special study of the psycho-social sciences.

In brief, then, the psycho-social sciences differ from the physical sciences in the nature of their subject-matter, in the sources of their knowledge about it, and in their own relation to it. Such regularities as they can observe are inconstant artifacts of the system which they study and are affected by their studies. They lack sources of knowledge on which other sciences rely; they are enriched by knowledge of a kind which other sciences would hate to have; and they are deprived of distance which other sciences regard as essential. None the less, they gather a body of tested knowledge and what they gather is significant to other sciences and their own as the findings of other sciences can never be. For it alone provides the basis for an epistemology which can illuminate what they and all their scientific colleagues are doing and can hope to do and a critique essential to the effective working and the intelligent use of humanity's most trusted instrument – science.

VII. Some Residual Enigmas

Substantial as is the contribution of the communication engineer to the understanding of our essentially communicative species, we should not overrate it. We credit ourselves on what seems to me incontrovertible evidence with complexities which the communication engineer cannot model.

That humans function in varying states of consciousness is the best-attested fact of human experience and is the only basis on which we credit each other with similar experience. In particular, the creative work attributable to scientists is widely attested to depend on the co-operation of several levels of consciousness. (Even the words I write appear on the paper before me from a level inaccessible to me and often express thoughts which surprise me and sometimes fail to convince my conscious mind.) Abnormal and disturbed relations between levels of consciousness have been extensively studied as psychopathology but normal and excellent functioning have as yet received little systematic attention.

The significance of this obscure field for the purpose of this paper is twofold. First, as I have already noted, it saddles us for good and ill with knowledge of our fellow-men different in kind from our knowledge of anything else, a fact pregnant with possibilities both for understanding and for error. Secondly, our belief in it underlies all our labours of communication. Scientists write books and politicians make speeches in the belief that it makes a difference to bring something to the conscious attention of others or even of oneself; and further, that this difference is partly the result of unconscious processes of reflection set in motion by a message which can only be received consciously. I see no difficulty in principle in conceiving the appreciative system as working at different levels, dependent for their proper functioning on being partly isolated from each other; but so far as I know, no communication engineer has attempted even the most speculative model of such an apparatus.

The second characteristic of humans, obvious but not yet modelled clearly by communication engineers, is the variety of the communication network in which they are involved. Each of us is bombarded by potential information from all manner of sources, from which we accept only what the current set of our attention and the current setting of our appreciative system allows us to notice and interpret. Only part of this input is in the highly pregnant form of words; and words need to be distinguished from other signals in ways we cannot yet fully describe. Of this verbal stream only a small fraction is beamed to us individually by an individual sender intent on communication; and even this small fraction is of many kinds. It may be the unilateral transfer of information, question, or order. It may be part of a verbal contest, in which each seeks to manipulate the appreciative system of the other, while guarding his own. Only a small fraction of this small fraction consists in exploration of a partly shared appreciative system with a view to reconciling and enlarging the systems of all the participants. Belief in the virtue of this last kind of communication underlies our most cherished convictions about human relations, education, the democratic process, and much else; and probably only this last fraction deserves the name of dialogue. We are only beginning to analyse these differences. Computers do not yet, I believe, engage in such dialogue with each other; and even science fiction, so far as I know, has not yet tried to chart the alarming results that might follow if they did. For I see no reason to suppose that any 'values' which computers might generate in such a process, however apt to 'computer nature', would bear any relation to the norms which the consensus of human societies seem to have been slowly evolving. So far the emergence of the computer as a human partner has not merely speeded the solution of the kind of problem that computers can solve but has begun to push still further into the background the more important problems which at present they cannot solve, notably the evolution of criteria for making multi-valued choices.

And this constitutes a third area of inquiry in which communication theory does not yet help us. To describe the process by which interests are generated and standards evolved as mediated by dialogue and reflection asserts nothing but the not yet accepted fact that the process involves more than the reactions of responsiveness. Yet even this cursory analysis seems to me to throw some light on the differences, often noticed, in the courses of development shown respectively by the values of science, ethics, politics, and art.

The only peculiarity of science as a human activity is that its values – its interests and standards of success – are those of the map-maker, not the map-user. The observation, so often repeated, that our age is richer in know-how than in know-what is only another way of saying that a map is no substitute for a journey. An age which does not know where it wants to go concentrates on the making of maps, just as, not knowing what it wants to buy, it concentrates on the making of money. 'Money,' wrote an economist, 'is dope, a tranquillizer against the effects of not knowing what to do' (Shackle, 1958). Science, similarly, is a tranquillizer against the effects of not knowing where to go. It would be silly to blame science for this and tragic to expect to get the whole answer from the map.

Yet the psycho-social scientist's map – and his alone – will remain incomplete, until it supplies some of the answer. For among the facts that he must represent none is more obvious than that men are incorrigible valuers. The enigmatic process by which interests are generated, standards evolved, and multi-valued choices made is his business *as a scientist*. To him – and to him alone – the activity of his fellow scientists is matter for study in its full complexity; and so is his own. He is condemned – or privileged – by the nature of his subject-matter to be always in some degree a participant observer. If this makes his methods and his validations different from those of the physical sciences, it is urgently important that the differences be clearly stated; and it is for him to state them.

The paths to knowledge in the three domains of science are significantly different. Those familiar with the paths in the earliest domain may recoil from the obscurity of those which penetrate the third. But they cannot avoid them.

For Science is human.

This paper was written in 1965 and has not previously been published.

REFERENCES

ABERCROMBIE, M. L. JOHNSON. 1960. *The Anatomy of Judgment.* London: Hutchinson.

EDDINGTON, SIR ARTHUR. 1949. *The Philosophy of Physical Science.* London: Cambridge University Press.

FRIEDMANN, W. 1959. *Law in a Changing Society.* London: Stevens.

GLUCKMAN, M. 1955. *The Judicial Process among the Barotse*. Manchester: Manchester University Press.

KELLER, HELEN. 1920. *The Story of my Life*. London: Hodder & Stoughton.

LANGER, SUSANNE. 1957. *Philosophy in a New Key*. Cambridge, Mass.: Harvard University Press.

POLANYI, M. 1958. Personal Knowledge. London: Routledge & Kegan Paul.

POLANYI, M. 1963. The Potential Theory of Adsorption. *Science*, Vol. 141, No. 3585, pp. 1010–13.

POPPER, K. 1957. *The Poverty of Historicism*. London: Routledge & Kegan Paul.

SHACKLE, G. L. S. 1958. The Economist's Model of Man. *Occupational Psychology*, Vol. 32, No. 3.

TINBERGEN, N. 1951. *The Study of Instinct*. Oxford: Clarendon Press.

VICKERS, G. 1964. The Psychology of Policy Making and Social Change. *British Journal of Psychology*, Vol. 110, No. 467.

VICKERS, G. 1965. *The Art of Judgment*. London: Chapman & Hall; New York: Basic Books.

WEAVER, W. 1948. Science and Complexity. *American Scientist*, Vol. 36, No. 4.

WERTHEIMER, M. 1959. *Productive Thinking*. New York: Harper & Row; London: Tavistock Publications, 1961.

Index

Index